Monologues from Shakespeare's First Folio for Younger Men: *The Tragedies*

The Applause Shakespeare Monologue Series

Other Shakespeare Titles From Applause

Once More unto the Speech Dear Friends
Volume One: The Comedies
Compiled and Edited with Commentary by Neil Freeman

Once More unto the Speech Dear Friends
Volume Two: The Histories
Compiled and Edited with Commentary by Neil Freeman

Once More unto the Speech Dear Friends
Volume Three: The Tragedies
Compiled and Edited with Commentary by Neil Freeman

The Applause First Folio in Modern Type
Prepared and Annotated by Neil Freeman

The Folio Texts
Prepared and Annotated by Neil Freeman, Each of the 36 plays of the
Applause First Folio in Modern Type individually bound

The Applause Shakespeare Library
Plays of Shakespeare Edited for Performance

Soliloquy: The Shakespeare Monologues

Monologues from Shakespeare's First Folio for Younger Men: *The Tragedies*

Compilation and Commentary by
Neil Freeman

Edited by
Paul Sugarman

APPLAUSE
THEATRE & CINEMA BOOKS
Guilford, Connecticut

APPLAUSE
THEATRE & CINEMA BOOKS

An imprint of Globe Pequot, the trade division of
The Rowman & Littlefield Publishing Group, Inc.
4501 Forbes Blvd., Ste. 200
Lanham, MD 20706
www.rowman.com

Distributed by NATIONAL BOOK NETWORK

Library of Congress Cataloging-in-Publication Data available

Library of Congress Control Number: 2021944367

ISBN 978-1-4930-5692-7 (paperback)
ISBN 978-1-4930-5693-4 (ebook)

♾️™ The paper used in this publication meets the minimum requirements of
American National Standard for Information Sciences—Permanence of Paper for
Printed Library Materials, ANSI/NISO Z39.48-1992

Dedication

Although Neil Freeman passed to that "undiscovered country" in 2015, his work continues to lead students and actors to a deeper understanding of Shakespeare's plays. With the exception of Shakespeare's words (and my humble foreword), the entirety of the material within these pages is Neil's. May these editions serve as a lasting legacy to a life of dedicated scholarship, and a great passion for Shakespeare.

Contents

FOREWORD

Paul Sugarman

Monologues from Shakespeare's First Folio presents the work of Neil Freeman, longtime champion of Shakespeare's First Folio, whose groundbreaking explorations into how first printings offered insights to the text in rehearsals, stage and in the classroom. This work continued with *Once More Unto the Speech Dear Friends: Monologues from Shakespeare's First Folio with Modern Text Versions for Comparison* where Neil collected over 900 monologues divided between the Comedy, History and Tragedy Published by Applause in three masterful volumes which present the original First Folio text side by side with the modern, edited version of the text. These volumes provide a massive amount of material and information. However both the literary scope, and the literal size of these volumes can be intimidating and overwhelming. This series' intent is to make the work more accessible by taking material from the encyclopediac original volumes and presenting it in an accessible workbook format.

To better focus the work for actors and students the texts are contrasted side by side with introductory notes before and commentary after to aid the exploration of the text. By comparing modern and First Folio printings, Neil points the way to gain new insights into Shakespeare's text. Editors over the centuries have "corrected" and updated the texts to make them "accessible," or "grammatically correct." In doing so they have lost vital clues and information that Shakespeare placed there for his actors. With the texts side by side, you can see where and why editors have made changes and what may have been lost in translation.

In addition to being divided into Histories, Comedies, and Tragedies, the original series further breaks down speeches by the character's designated gender, also indicating speeches appropriate for any gender. Drawing from this example, this series breaks down each original volume into four workbooks: speeches for Women of all ages, Younger Men, Older Men and Any Gender. Gender is naturally fluid for Shakespeare's characters since during his time, ALL of the characters were portrayed by males. Contemporary productions of Shakespeare commonly switch character genders (Prospero has become Prospera), in addition to presenting single gender, reverse gender and gender non-specific productions. There are certainly characters and speeches where the gender is immaterial, hence the inclusion of a volume of speeches for Any Gender. This was something that Neil had indicated in the original volumes; we are merely following his example.

Once More Unto the Speech Dear Friends was a culmination of Neil's dedicated efforts to make the First Folio more accessible and available to readers and to illuminate for actors the many clues within the Folio text, as originally published. The material in this book is drawn from that work and retains Neil's British spelling of words (i.e. capitalisation) and his extensive commentary on each speech. Neil went on to continue this work as a master teacher of Shakespeare with another series of Shakespeare editions, his 'rhythm texts' and the ebook that he published on Apple Books, *The Shakespeare Variations.*

Neil published on his own First Folio editions of the plays in modern type which were the basis the Folio Texts series published by Applause of all 36 plays in the First Folio. These individual editions all have extensive notes on the changes that modern editions had made. This material was then combined to create a complete reproduction of the First Folio in modern type, *The Applause First Folio of Shakespeare in Modern Type.* These editions make the First Folio more accessible than ever before. The examples in this book demonstrate how the clues from the First Folio will give insights to understanding and performing these speeches and why it is a worthwhile endeavour to discover the riches in the First Folio.

PREFACE AND BRIEF BACKGROUND TO THE FIRST FOLIO

WHY ANOTHER SERIES OF SOLILOQUY BOOKS?

There has been an enormous change in theatre organisation recent in the last twenty years. While the major large-scale companies have continued to flourish, many small theatre companies have come into being, leading to

- much doubling
- cross gender casting, with many one time male roles now being played legitimately by/as women in updated time-period productions
- young actors being asked to play leading roles at far earlier points in their careers

All this has meant actors should be able to demonstrate enormous flexibility rather than one limited range/style. In turn, this has meant

- a change in audition expectations
- actors are often expected to show more range than ever before
- often several shorter audition speeches are asked for instead of one or two longer ones
- sometimes the initial auditions are conducted in a shorter amount of time

Thus, to stay at the top of the game, the actor needs more knowledge of what makes the play tick, especially since

- early plays demand a different style from the later ones
- the four genres (comedy, history, tragedy, and the peculiar romances) all have different acting/textual requirements
- parts originally written for the older, more experienced actors again require a different approach from those written for the younger

ones, as the young roles, especially the female ones, were played by young actors extraordinarily skilled in the arts of rhetoric

There's now much more knowledge of how the original quarto and folio texts can add to the rehearsal exploration/acting and directing process as well as to the final performance.

Each speech is made up of four parts

- a background to the speech, placing it in the context of the play, and offering line length and an approximate timing to help you choose what might be right for any auditioning occasion
- a modern text version of the speech, with the sentence structure clearly delineated side by side with
- a folio version of the speech, where modern texts changes to the capitalization, spelling and sentence structure can be plainly seen
- a commentary explaining the differences between the two texts, and in what way the original setting can offer you more information to explore

Thus if they wish, **beginners** can explore just the background and the modern text version of the speech.

An actor experienced in exploring the Folio can make use of the background and the Folio version of the speech

And those wanting to know as many details as possible and how they could help define the deft stepping stones of the arc of the speech can use all four elements on the page.

The First Folio

(FOR LIST OF CURRENT REPRODUCTIONS SEE BIBLIOGRAPHY

The end of 1623 saw the publication of the justifiably famed First Folio (F1). The single volume, published in a run of approximately 1,000 copies at the princely sum of one pound (a tremendous risk, considering that a single play would sell at no more than six pence, one fortieth of F1's price, and that the annual salary of a schoolmaster was only ten pounds), contained thirty-six plays.

The manuscripts from which each F1 play would be printed came from a variety of sources. Some had already been printed. Some came from the playhouse complete with production details. Some had no theatrical input at all, but were handsomely copied out and easy to read. Some were supposedly very messy, complete with first draft scribbles and crossings out. Yet, as Charlton Hinman, the revered dean of First Folio studies describes F1 in the Introduction to the Norton Facsimile:

> It is of inestimable value for what it is, for what it contains. For here are preserved the masterworks of the man universally recognized as our greatest writer; and preserved, as Ben Jonson realized at the time of the original publication, not for an age but for all time.

WHAT DOES F1 REPRESENT?

- texts prepared for actors who rehearsed three days for a new play and one day for one already in the repertoire
- written in a style (rhetoric incorporating debate) so different from ours (grammatical) that many modern alterations based on grammar (or poetry) have done remarkable harm to the rhetorical/debate quality of the original text and thus to interpretations of characters at key moments of stress.
- written for an acting company the core of which steadily grew older, and whose skills and interests changed markedly over twenty years as well as for an audience whose make-up and interests likewise changed as the company grew more experienced

The whole is based upon supposedly the best documents available at the time, collected by men closest to Shakespeare throughout his career, and brought to a single printing house whose errors are now widely understood - far more than those of some of the printing houses that produced the original quartos.

TEXTUAL SOURCES FOR THE AUDITION SPEECHES
Individual modern editions consulted in the preparation of the Modern Text version of the speeches are listed in the Bibliography under the separate headings 'The Complete Works in Compendium Format' and ' The Complete Works in Separate Individual Volumes.' Most of the modern versions of the speeches are a compilation of several of these texts. However, all modern act, scene and/or line numbers refer the reader to The Riverside Shakespeare, in my opinion still the best of the complete works despite the excellent compendiums that have been published since.

The First Folio versions of the speeches are taken from a variety of already published sources, including not only all the texts listed in the 'Photostatted Reproductions in Compendium Format' section of the Bibliography, but also earlier, individually printed volumes, such as the twentieth century editions published under the collective title *The Facsimiles of Plays from The First Folio of Shakespeare* by Faber & Gwyer, and the nineteenth century editions published on behalf of The New Shakespeare Society.

INTRODUCTION

So, congratulations, you've got an audition, and for a Shakespeare play no less.

You've done all your homework, including, hopefully , reading the whole play to see the full range and development of the character.

You've got an idea of the character, the situation in which you/it finds itself (the given circumstance s); what your/its needs are (objectives/ intentions); and what you intend to do about them (action /tactics).

You've looked up all the unusual words in a good dictionary or glossary; you've turned to a well edited modern edition to find out what some of the more obscure references mean.

And those of you who understand metre and rhythm have worked on the poetic values of the speech, and you are word perfect . . .

. . . and yet it's still not working properly and/or you feel there's more to be gleaned from the text , but you're not sure what that something is or how to go about getting at it; in other words, all is not quite right, yet.

THE KEY QUESTION

What text have you been working with - a good modern text or an 'original' text, that is a copy of one of the first printings of the play?

If it's a modern text, no matter how well edited (and there are some splendid single copy editions available, see the Bibliography for further details), despite all the learned information offered, it's not surprising you feel somewhat at a loss, for there is a huge difference between the original printings (the First Folio, and the individual quartos, see

Appendix 1 for further details) and any text prepared after 1700 right up to the most modern of editions. All the post 1700 texts have been tidied-up for the modern reader to ingest silently, revamped according to the rules of correct grammar, syntax and poetry. However the 'originals' were prepared for actors speaking aloud playing characters often in a great deal of emotional and/or intellectual stress, and were set down on paper according to the very flexible rules of rhetoric and a seemingly very cavalier attitude towards the rules of grammar, and syntax, and spelling, and capitalisation, and even poetry.

Unfortunately, because of the grammatical and syntactical standardisation in place by the early 1700's, many of the quirks and oddities of the origin also have been dismissed as 'accidental' - usually as compositor error either in deciphering the original manuscript, falling prey to their own particular idosyncracies, or not having calculated correctly the amount of space needed to set the text. Modern texts dismiss the possibility that these very quirks and oddities may be by Shakespeare, hearing his characters in as much difficulty as poor Peter Quince is in *A Midsummer Night's Dream* (when he, as the Prologue, terrified and struck down by stage fright, makes a huge grammatical hash in introducing his play 'Pyramus and Thisbe' before the aristocracy, whose acceptance or otherwise, can make or break him)

> If we offend, it is with our good will.
> That you should think, we come not to offend,
> But with good will.
> > To show our simple skill,
> That is the true beginning of our end .
> Consider then, we come but in despite.
> We do not come, as minding to content you ,
> Our true intent is.
> > All for your delight
> We are not here.
> > That you should here repent you,

The Actors are at hand; and by their show,
You shall know all, that you are like to know.

(A Midsummer Night's Dream)

In many other cases in the complete works what was originally printed is equally 'peculiar,' but, unlike Peter Quince , these peculiarities are usually regularised by most modern texts.

However, this series of volumes is based on the belief - as the following will show - that most of these 'peculiarities' resulted from Shakespeare setting down for his actors the stresses, trials, and tribulations the characters are experiencing as they think and speak, and thus are theatrical gold-dust for the actor, director, scholar, teacher, and general reader alike.

THE FIRST ESSENTIAL DIFFERENCE BETWEEN THE TWO TEXTS

THINKING

A **modern** text can show

- the story line
- your character's conflict with the world at large
- your character's conflict with certain individuals within that world

but because of the very way an 'original' text was set, it can show you all this plus one key extra, the very thing that makes big speeches what they are

- the conflict within the character

WHY?

Any good playwright writes about characters in stressful situations who are often in a state of conflict not only with the world around them and the people in that world, but also within themselves. And you probably know from personal experience that when these conflicts occur people do not necessarily utter the most perfect of grammatical/poetic/ syntactic statements, phrases, or sentences. Joy and delight, pain and sorrow often come sweeping through in the way things are said, in the incoherence of the phrases, the running together of normally disassociated ideas, and even in the sounds of the words themselves.

The tremendous advantage of the period in which Shakespeare was setting his plays down on paper and how they first appeared in print was that when characters were rational and in control of self and situation, their phrasing and sentences (and poetic structure) would appear to be quite normal even to a modern eye - but when things were going wrong, so sentences and phrasing (and poetic structure) would become highly erratic. But the Quince type eccentricities are rarely allowed to stand. Sadly, in tidying, most modern texts usually make the text far too clean, thus setting rationality when none originally existed.

THE SECOND ESSENTIAL DIFFERENCE BETWEEN THE TWO TEXTS

SPEAKING, ARGUING, DEBATING

Having discovered what and how you/your character is thinking is only the first stage of the work - you/it then have to speak aloud, in a society that absolutely loved to speak - and not only speak ideas (content) but to speak entertainingly so as to keep listeners enthralled (and this was especially so when you have little content to offer and have to mask it somehow - think of today 's television adverts and political spin doctors as a parallel and you get the picture). Indeed one of the Elizabethan 'how to win an argument' books was very precise about this - George Puttenham, *The Art of English Poesie* (1589).

A: ELIZABETHAN SCHOOLING

All educated classes could debate/argue at the drop of a hat, for both boys (in 'petty-schools') and girls (by books and tutors) were trained in what was known overall as the art of rhetoric, which itself was split into three parts

- first, how to distinguish the real from false appearances/outward show (think of the three caskets in *The Merchant of Venice* where the language on the gold and silver caskets enticingly, and deceptively, seems to offer hopes of great personal rewards that are dashed when the language is carefully explored, whereas once the apparent threat on the lead casket is carefully analysed the reward therein is the greatest that could be hoped for)
- second, how to frame your argument on one of 'three great grounds'; honour/morality; justice/legality; and, when all else fails, expedience/practicality.
- third, how to order and phrase your argument so winsomely that your audience will vote for you no matter how good the opposition - and there were well over two hundred rules and variations by which winning could be achieved, all of which had to be assimilated before a child's education was considered over and done with.

B: THINKING ON YOUR FEET: I.E. THE QUICK, DEFT , RAPID MODIFICATION OF EACH TINY THOUGHT

The Elizabethan/therefore your character/therefore you were also trained to explore and modify your thoughts as you spoke - never would you see a sentence in its entirety and have it perfectly worked out in your mind before you spoke (unless it was a deliberately written, formal public declaration, as with the Officer of the Court in The Winter' s Tale, reading the charges against Hermione). Thus after uttering your very first phrase, you might expand it, or modify it, deny it, change it, and so on throughout the whole sentence and speech.

From the poet Samuel Coleridge Taylor there is a wonderful description of how Shakespeare puts thoughts together like "a serpent twisting and untwisting in its own strength," that is, with one thought springing out of the one previous. Treat each new phrase as a fresh unravelling of the serpent's coil. What is discovered (and therefore said) is only revealed as the old coil/phrase disappears revealing a new coil in its place. The new coil is the new thought. The old coil moves/disappears because the previous phrase is finished with as soon as it is spoken.

C: MODERN APPLICATION

It is very rarely we speak dispassionately in our 'real' lives, after all thoughts give rise to feelings, feelings give rise to thoughts, and we usually speak both together - unless

1/ we're trying very hard for some reason to control ourselves and not give ourselves away

2/ or the volcano of emotions·within us is so strong that we cannot control ourselves, and feelings swamp thoughts

3/ and sometimes whether deliberately or unconsciously we colour words according to our feelings; the humanity behind the words so revealed is instantly understandable.

D: HOW THE ORIGINAL TEXTS NATURALLY ENHANCE/ UNDERSCORE THIS CONTROL OR RELEASE

The amazing thing about the way all Elizabethan/early Jacobean texts were first set down (the term used to describe the printed words on the page being 'orthography'), is that it was flexible, it allowed for such variations to be automatically set down without fear of grammatical repercussion.

So if Shakespeare heard Juliet's nurse working hard to try to convince Juliet that the Prince's nephew Juliet is being forced to (bigamously) marry, instead of setting the everyday normal

'O he's a lovely gentleman'

which the modern texts HAVE to set, the first printings were permitted to set

'O hee's a Lovely Gentleman'

suggesting that something might be going on inside the Nurse that causes her to release such excessive extra energy.

E: BE CAREFUL

This needs to be stressed very carefully: the orthography doesn't dictate to you/force you to accept exactly what it means. The orthography simply suggests you might want to explore this moment further or more deeply.

In other words, simply because of the flexibility with which the Elizabethans/Shakespeare could set down on paper what they heard in their minds or wanted their listeners to hear, in addition to all the modern acting necessities of character - situation, objective, intention, action, and tactics the original Shakespeare texts offer pointers to where feelings (either emotional or intellectual, or when combined together as passion, both) are also evident.

SUMMARY

BASIC APPROACH TO THE SPEECHES SHOWN BELOW

(after reading the 'background')

1/ first use the modem version shown in the first column: by doing so you can discover

- the basic plot line of what's happening to the character, and
- the first set of conflicts/obstacles impinging on the character as a result of the situation or actions of other characters
- the supposed grammatical and poetical correctnesses of the speech

2/ then you can explore

- any acting techniques you'd apply to any modem soliloquy, including establishing for the character
- the given circumstances of the scene
- their outward state of being (who they are sociologically, etc.)
- their intentions and objectives
- the resultant action and tactics they decide to pursue

3/ when this is complete, turn to the First Folio version of the text, shown on the facing page: this will help you discover and explore

- the precise thinking and debating process so essential to an understanding of any Shakespeare text
- the moments when the text is NOT grammatically or poetically as correct as the modern texts would have you believe, which will in tum help you recognise
- the moments of conflict and struggle stemming from within the character itself
- the sense of fun and enjoyment the Shakespeare language nearly always offers you no matter how dire the situation

4/ should you wish to further explore even more the differences between the two texts, the commentary that follows discusses how the First Folio has been changed, and what those alterations might mean for the human arc of the speech

NOTES ON HOW THESE SPEECHES ARE SET UP

For each of the speeches the first page will include the Background on the speech and other information including number of lines, approximate timing and who is addressed. Then will follow a spread which shows the modern text version on the left and the First Folio version on the right, followed by a page of Commentary.

PROBABLE TIMING: (shown on the Background page before the speeches begin, set below the number of lines) 0.45 = a forty-five second speech

SYMBOLS & ABBREVIATIONS IN THE COMMENTARY AND TEXT

F: the First Folio

mt.: modern texts

F # followed by a number: the number of the sentence under discussion in the First Folio version of the speech, thus F #7 would refer to the seventh sentence

mt. # followed by a numb er: the number of the sentence under discussion in the modern text version of the speech, thus mt. #5 would refer to the fifth sentence

 # /#, (e.g. 3/7): the first number refers to the number of capital letters in the passage under discussion; the second refers to the number of long spellings therein

within a quotation from the speech: / indicates where one verse line ends and a fresh one starts

[ ] : set around words in both texts when F1 sets one word , mt another

{ } : some minor alteration has been made, in a speech built up, where, a word or phrase will be changed, added, or removed

{†} : this symbol shows where a sizeable part of the text is omitted

TERMS FOUND IN THE COMMENTARY
OVERALL

1/ **orthography**: the capitalization, spellings, punctuation of the First Folio
SIGNS OF IMPORTANT DISCOVERIES/ARGUMENTS WITHIN A FIRST FOLIO SPEECH

2/ **major punctuation**: colons and semicolons: since the Shakespeare texts are based so much on the art of debate and argument, the importance of F1's major punctuation must not be underestimated, for both the semi-colon (;) and colon (:) mark a moment of importance for the character, either for itself, as a moment of discovery or revelation, or as a key point in a discussion, argument or debate that it wishes to impress upon other characters onstage

as a rule of thumb:

a/ the more frequent colon (:) suggests that whatever the power of the point discovered or argued, the character is not side-tracked and can continue with the argument - as such, the colon can be regarded as a **logical** connection

b/ the far less frequent semicolon (;) suggests that because of the power inherent in the point discovered or argued, the character is side-tracked and momentarily loses the argument and falls back into itself or can only continue the argument with great difficulty - as such, the semicolon should be regarded as an **emotional** connection

3/ **surround phrases**: phrase(s) surrounded by major punctuation, or a combination of major punctuation and the end or beginning of a sentence: thus these phrases seem to be of especial importance for both character and speech, well worth exploring as key to the argument made and /or emotions released

DIALOGUE NOT FOUND IN THE FIRST FOLIO

∞ set where modern texts add dialogue from a quarto text which has not been included in Fl

A LOOSE RULE OF THUMB TO THE THINKING PROCESS OF A FIRST FOLIO CHARACTER

1/ mental discipline/**intellect**: a section where capitals dominate suggests that the intellectual reason ing behind what is being spoken or discovered is of more concern than the personal response beneath it

2/ feelings/**emotions**: a section where long spellings dominate suggests that the personal response to what is being spoken or discovered is of more concern than the intellectual reasoning behind it

3/ **passion**: a section where both long spellings and capitals are present in almost equal proportions suggests that both mind and emotion/feelings are inseparable, and thus the character is speaking passionately

SIGNS OF LESS THAN GRAMMATICAL THINKING WITHIN A FIRST FOLIO SPEECH

1/ **onrush**: sometimes thoughts are coming so fast that several topics are joined together as one long sentence suggesting that the F character's mind is working very quickly, or that his/her emotional state is causing some concern: most mod ern texts split such a sentence into several grammatically correct parts (the opening speech of *As You Like It* is a fine example, where F's long 18 line opening sentence is split into six): while the modern texts' resetting may be syntactically correct, the F moment is nowhere near as calm as the revisions suggest

2/ **fast-link**: sometimes F shows thoughts moving so quickly for a character that the connecting punctuation between disparate topics is merely a comma, suggesting that there is virtually no pause in springing from one idea to the next: unfortunately most modern texts rarely allow this to stand, instead replacing the obviously disturbed comma with a grammatical period, once more creating calm that it seems the original texts never intended to show

FIRST FOLIO SIGNS OF WHEN VERBAL GAME PLAYING HAS TO STOP

1/ **non-embellished:** a section with neither capitals nor long spellings suggests that what is being discovered or spoken is so important to the character that there is no time to guss it up with vocal or mental excesses: an unusual moment of self-control

2/ **short sentence:** coming out of a society where debate was second nature, man y of Shakespeare's characters speak in long sentences in which ideas are stated, explored, redefined and summarized all before moving onto the next idea in the argument, discovery or debate: the longer sentence is the sign of a rhetorically trained mind used to public speaking (oratory), but at times an idea or discovery is so startling or inevitable that length is either unnecessary or impossible to maintain : hence the occasional very important short sentence suggests that there is no time for the niceties of oratorical adornment with which to sugar the pill - verbal games are at an end and now the basic core of the issue must be faced

3/ **monosyllabic:** with English being composed of two strands, the polysyllabic (stemming from French, Italian, Latin and Greek), and the monosyllabic (from the Anglo-Saxon), each strand has two distinct functions: the polysyllabic words are often used when there is time for fanciful elaboration and rich description (which could be described as 'excessive rhetoric') while the monosyllabic occur when, literally, there is no other way of putting a basic question or comment - Juliet's "Do you love me? I know thou wilt say aye" is a classic example of both monosyllables and non-embellishment: with monosyllables, only the naked truth is being spoken, nothing is hidden

Monologues from Shakespeare's First Folio for Younger Men: *The Tragedies*

The Lamentable Tragedie of Titus Andronicus

Saturninus

Noble Patricians, Patrons of my right,
1.1.1. - -8

Bassianus

Romaines, Friends, Followers,
1.1.9 - 17

Background: two brothers, rivals to succeed their father, the recently deceased Emperor of Rome, appeal to the public at large for their support: each is supported by followers and 'drums and colours', suggesting the possibility of conflict: as the elder, Saturninus begins

Style: both, public address in the open air to a large group of people

Where: unspecified, but a public square in Rome

To Whom: a large group, comprised of Tribunes, Senators, and followers for each of the candidates

Saturninus/ # of Lines: 8 • Probable Timing: 0.30 minutes

Bassianus/ # of Lines: 9 • Probable Timing: 0.30 minutes

Take Note: There is a marked difference between the two brothers-Saturninus is logical in sentence structure and in terms of spelling relatively self-contained. Bassianus is more openly passionate (the one long sentence scattered with extra spellings) yet still can make all the necessary logical stepping stones via the major punctuation

Saturninus

1　Noble patricians, patrons of my right,
　　Defend the justice of my cause with arms;
　　And, countrymen, my loving followers,
　　Plead my successive title with your swords.

2　I [am his] first born son, that was the last
　　That ware the imperial diadem of Rome,
　　Then let my father's honors live in me,
　　Nor wrong mine age with this indignity.

Bassianus

1　Romans, friends, followers, favorers of my right,
　　If ever Bassianus, Cæsar's son,
　　Were gracious in the eyes of royal Rome,
　　Keep then this passage to the Capitol,
　　And suffer not dishonor to approach
　　Th'imperial seat, to virtue consecrate,
　　To justice, continence, and nobility;
　　But let desert in pure election shine,
　　And, Romans, fight for freedom in your choice.

Saturninus

1   Noble Patricians, Patrons of my right,
     Defend the justice of my Cause with Armes.

2   And Countrey-men, my loving Followers,
     Pleade my Successive Title with your Swords.

3   I [was the] first borne Sonne, that was the last
     That wore the Imperiall Diadem of Rome :
     Then let my Fathers Honours live in me,
     Nor wrong mine Age with this indignitie.

Bassianus

1   Romaines, Friends, Followers,
     Favourers of my Right :
     If ever Bassianus, Cæsars Sonne,
     Were gracious in the eyes of Royall Rome,
     Keepe then this passage to the Capitoll :
     And suffer not Dishonour to approach
     Th'Imperiall Seate to Vertue : consecrate
     To Justice, Continence, and Nobility :
     But let Desert in pure Election shine ;
     And Romanes, fight for Freedome in your Choice.

- F's two sentence opening marks more clearly than the (longer) modern text Saturninus' clever appeal to two different classes, first the 'Noble Patricians', and only then the lesser 'Countey-men' in general

- the appalling incitement to civil war - 'Armes' and 'Swords' - seems determinedly intellectual (a 9 capital lead-up accompanied by just 3 long spellings)

- and the ensuing argument is all weighted on his father's merits (all four long spellings) rather than his own

- though one long sentence, F clearly outlines each stage of Bassianus' argument with the five pieces of major punctuation (4 : and 1 ;): sadly, few modern texts maintain them – thus removing his fine sense of oratory

- unlike his brother, Bassianus' capitals refer to the abstract values of 'Vertue','Justice', 'Continence', 'Nobility', 'Desert', and his plea to his own, not his father's 'Right'

- the three key surround phrases that finish up the speech (starting from 'consecrate', ending the fourth line from the bottom) all point to Bassianus' love of Rome and democracy, and thus the honorable nature of his plea

- yet despite the intellect, the frequent long spellings – proportionately more than for his brother - show there are strong emotions burning within him

The Lamentable Tragedie of Titus Andronicus

Aaron

Now climbeth Tamora Olympus toppe,
2.1.1 - 24

Background: the first speech in the play for Aaron, Tamora's lover: as such, it is self-explanatory

Style: solo

Where: unspecified, but probably in or near the palace

To Whom: self, and direct audience address

# of Lines: 24

Probable Timing: 1.15 minutes

Take Note: The modern text resetting of the F sentence structure turns what was originally a relatively uncontrolled personal release full of passion (delight perhaps?) into a far neater and tidier analytical exposition.

Aaron

1   Now climbeth Tamora Olympus' top,
     Safe out of fortune's shot, and sits aloft,
     Secure of thunder's crack or lightning flash,
     Advanc'd [above] pale envy's threat'ning reach.

2   As when the golden sun salutes the morn,
     And having gilt the ocean with his beams,
     Gallops the zodiac in his glistering coach,
     And overlooks the highest peering hills:
     So Tamora.

3   Upon her wit doth earthly honor wait,
     And virtue stoops and trembles at her frown;
     Then, Aaron, arm thy heart, and fit thy thoughts,
     To mount aloft with thy imperial mistress,
     And mount her pitch, whom thou in triumph long
     Hast prisoner held, fett'red in amorous chains,
     And faster bound to Aaron's charming eyes,
     [Than] is Prometheus tied to Caucasus.

4   Away with slavish weeds and [servile] thoughts!

5   I will be bright, and shine in pearl and gold,
     To wait upon this new made emperess.

6   To wait said I?   to wanton with this queen,
     This goddess, this [Semiramis], this [nymph],
     This siren that will charm Rome's Saturnine,
     And see his shipwrack and his commonweal's

Aaron

1   Now climbeth Tamora Olympus toppe,
Safe out of Fortunes shot, and sits aloft,
Secure of Thunders cracke or lightning flash,
Advanc'd [about] pale envies threatning reach :
As when the golden Sunne salutes the morne,
And having gilt the Ocean with his beames,
Gallops the Zodiacke in his glistering Coach,
And over-lookes the highest piering hills :
So Tamora :
Upon her wit doth earthly honour waite,
And vertue stoopes and trembles at her frowne.

2   Then Aaron arme thy hart, and fit thy thoughts,
To mount aloft with thy Emperiall Mistris,
And mount her pitch, whom thou in triumph long
Hast prisoner held, fettred in amorous chaines,
And faster bound to Aarons charming eyes,
[Then] is Prometheus ti'de to Caucasus.

3   Away with slavish weedes, and [idle] thoughts,
I will be bright and shine in Pearle and Gold,
To waite upon this new made Empresse.

4   To waite said I?

5   To wanton with this Queene,
This Goddesse, this [Semerimis], this [Queene],
This Syren, that will charme Romes Saturnine,
And see his shipwracke, and his Common weales.

• the speech is extremely passionate (26/26 in twenty-four lines)

• the single surround phrase " : So Tamora:" sums up the sole focus of his world and hopes

• the two short moments where capitals and long-spellings don't match are the two emotional lines ending the long F sentence #1 with his unabated admiration for Tamora's current power (0/4); and the wonderful intellectual self-assessment as to how inextricably sexually bound to him she is (the last two lines of sentence #2, 3/0)

• the long eleven line opening F sentence all centres on Tamora, and allows for a wonderful passionate build: modern texts have broken it down into mt.. #1-2 and the first two lines of #3, thus reducing the release and drive, and further . . .

• whereas in F sentence #2 Aaron now focuses his attention purely on himself, the modern rewrite has split this focus and weakened his drive, the first two lines now being about Tamora and only then turning towards himself

• similarly, the onrush of F sentence #3 allows him his due moment of passionate celebration, whereas the modern text's splitting it into #4-5 sets up the response as far more calculating

• and the celebration of the unusually short F sentence #4 "To waite said I?" allows him to a more pointed and concentrated moment in which to dream and revel before moving onto the sensuality of the last sentence: modern texts somewhat gut this by jamming F sentences #4-5 together

The Lamentable Tragedie of Titus Andronicus

Aaron

Sooner this sword shall plough thy bowels up.
between 4.2.87 - 111

Background: unbeknownst until the birth of the child, Aaron has sired a son on Tamora, and because of the child's colour it is obvious he is the father and not her husband Saturninus: fearful of reprisals Tamora has had their son brought to Aaron with orders to kill it, an order seconded by both Tamora's adult children: the following is triggered by Demetrius' 'Ile broach the Tadpole on my Rapiers point:/Nurse give it me, my sword shall soone dispatch it': one note, perhaps the nurse is holding the baby, or even Aaron himself

Style: address to two men, in front of one other person

Where: unspecified, but somewhere in or near the palace

To Whom: Tamora's sons Demetrius and Chiron, in front of the Nurse who brought the baby, and the baby

# of Lines: 24

Probable Timing: 1.15 minutes

Take Note: The control that the modern text Aaron seems to display throughout the scene is not supported by F's sentence structure and/or orthography. Though the opening three sentences match, once Aaron starts to heap the insults on the boys' heads (after the first colon of F sentence #3, start of mt.. sentence #5) intellect gives way to highly personal feelings.

Aaron

1   Sooner this sword shall plough thy bowels up.

2   Stay, [murderous] villains, will you kill your brother?

3   Now, by the burning tapers of the sky,
    That shone so brightly when this boy was got,
    He dies upon my [scimitar's] sharp point,
    That touches this my first-born son and heir!

4   I tell you younglings, not Enceladus,
    With all his threat'ning band of Typhon's brood,
    Nor great Alcides, nor the god of war,
    Shall seize this prey out of his father's hands.

5   What, what, ye sanguine, shallow harted boys!
    Ye white-[lim'd] walls! ye alehouse painted signs!

6   Coal black is better [than]another hue,
    In that it scorns to bear another hue;
    For all the water in the ocean
    Can never turn the swan's black legs to white,
    Although she lave them hourly in the flood.

7   Tell the Empress from me, I am of age
    To keep mine own, excuse it how she can.

---

8   My mistress is my mistress, this myself,
    The vigor and the picture of my youth:
    This before all the world do I prefer,
    This maugre all the world will I keep safe,
    Or some of you shall smoke for it in Rome.

Aaron

1   Sooner this sword shall plough thy bowels up.

2   Stay [murtherous] villaines, will you kill your brother?

3   Now by the burning Tapers of the skie,
    That sh'one so brightly when this Boy was got,
    He dies upon my [Semitars] sharpe point,
    That touches this my first borne sonne and heire.

4   I tell you young-lings, not Enceladus
    With all his threatning band of Typhons broode,
    Nor great Alcides, nor the God of warre,
    Shall ceaze this prey out of his fathers hands :
    What, what, ye sanguine shallow harted Boyes,
    Ye white-[limb'd] walls, ye Ale-house painted signes,
    Cole-blacke is better [then] another hue,
    In that it scornes to beare another hue :
    For all the water in the Ocean,
    Can never turne the Swans blacke legs to white,
    Although she lave them hourely in the flood :
    Tell the Empresse from me, I am of age
    To keepe mine owne, excuse it how she can.

5   My mistris is my mistris : this my selfe,
    The vigour, and the picture of my youth :
    This, before all the world do I preferre,
    This mauger all the world will I keepe safe,
    Or some of you shall smoake for it in Rome.

- there is a deceptive calm to the opening one line sentence (0/0), and even in the second equally unusually short F sentence #2 with just the one long-spelled 'villaines' (an insult to which Aaron returns a little later). Not surprisingly passion suddenly breaks through in sentence F #3 (3/4) finishing with a highly emotional cluster of long spellings 'my first borne sonne and heire'

- for a moment it seems if Aaron can recover for, thanks to the classical allusions rife in the opening four lines of F sentence #4, intellect seems to dominate emotion (4/2)

- but the insult of 'young-lings' a reference at best to an inferior fish, at worst to something sexually unpleasant (spoiled by the modern text resetting the more recogniseable 'younglings') paves the way for Aaron's act of double defiance – the protestation that 'Cole-blacke is better than another hue' and refusal to follow ('to keepe mine owne') Tamora's wishes to get rid of or kill the child, and the remainder of the speech is highly personal (6/16 in 14 lines)

- and not surprisingly F (#4) sets this release of emotion as one long sentence, the drive of which most modern texts deflate by splitting it into four

- Aaron's act of defining of the world as he sees it and will preserve it, i.e. an 'Empresse' (Tamora) is still his 'mistris', and his new born son is his sole concern is supported by the only surround phrases in the speech which opens the first two lines of the last sentence, F #5, viz.

  " . My mistris is my mistris : this my selfe,/The vigour, and the picture of my youth : "

The Tragedie of
Romeo and Juliet
Benvolio

At this same auncient Feast of Capulets
between 1.2.82 - 99

Background: having promised his aunt and uncle that as regards Romeo 'Ile know his greevance or be much denide', Benvolio has discovered that Romeo is suffering the pangs of unrequited love: then, having learned that Rosaline, the lady Romeo is being spurned by, will be at the enemy Capulet's party that night, Benvolio proposes an adventure

Style: as part of a two-handed scene

Where: the street

To Whom: Romeo

# of Lines: 12

Probable Timing: 0.40 minutes

Take Note: Mercutio's later description of Benvolio as a hothead seems to be borne out by F's slight onrush, the two extra breath-thoughts in the last two lines and the (possible) very strange last line.

Benvolio

1   At this same ancient feast of Capulet's
    Sups the fair Rosaline whom thou so loves,
    With all the admired beauties of Verona .

2   Go thither, and with unattainted eye,
    Compare her face with some that I shall show,
    And I will make thee think thy swan a crow.

---

3   {†}   {Y}ou saw her fair, none else being by,
    Herself pois'd with herself in either eye ;
    But in that crystal scales, let there be weigh'd
    Your lady's love against some other maid
    That I will show you shining at this feast,
    And she [shall scant show well] that now [seems] best

Benvolio

1　At this same auncient Feast of Capulets
　　Sups the faire Rosaline, whom thou so loves:
　　With all the admired Beauties of Verona,
　　Go thither and with unattainted eye,
　　Compare her face with some that I shall show,
　　And I will make thee thinke thy Swan a Crow.

2　{†}　　　　　　{Y}ou saw her faire, none else being by,
　　Herselfe poys'd with herselfe in either eye:
　　But in that Christall scales, let there be waid,
　　Your Ladies love against some other Maid
　　That I will show you, shining at this Feast,
　　And she [shew scant shell, well], that now [shewes] best.

• F#1's two unembellished lines "Go thither and with unat-tainted eye, /Compare her face with some that I shall show,', supported by F #2's 'That I will show you, shining at this Feast' point to the possible seriousness of Benvolio's attempt to deflect Romeo's current impotent adulation (an attempt not to lose his friend/cousin to a woman perhaps?)

• while F #1 starts intellectually (5/2, first three lines) and moves into the unembellished calm discussed above, it ends passionately (2/1), and moves straight into emotion as he demeans Rosaline (0/4, F #2's first two lines), while the final suggestion he can show women better than Rosaline is once more stoutly intellectual (4/2, the last four lines)

The Tragedie of Romeo and Juliet

Romeo

{I have not graced my}bed to night
between 2.3.42 - 64

Background: immediately on leaving Juliet, Romeo has rushed to Frier Lawrence for help in marrying Juliet, but before he can get the words out, since he admits that he 'hath not been in bed to night' but 'the sweeter rest was mine' the Frier exclaims 'god pardon sin: wast thou with Rosaline', which triggers the following

Style: as part of a two-handed scene

Where: the fields close to the Frier's cell

To Whom: Frier Lawrence

# of Lines: 17

Probable Timing: 0.55 minutes

Take Note: The speech is a wonderful mix of self-control (the unembellished F #1, F #3 and parts of F #5); determination (the surround phrases); pussy-footing around; and finally the actual request for the Frier to marry Juliet and himself, F #4 and #5); onrush in which the surround phrases are contained (however, most modern texts create far more control than originally set, with F #4 being split in two by, and F #5 into three); and emotion (4/9 overall).

Romeo

1   {I have not graced my} bed to night {-}
     {†}   the sweeter rest was mine.

---

2   With Rosaline ? my ghostly father , no;
     I have forgot that name, and that name's woe.

---

3   I have been feasting with mine enemy,
     Where on a sudden one hath wounded me
     That's by me wounded; both our remedies
     Within thy help and holy physic lies.

4   I bear no hatred, blessed man: for lo
     My intercession likewise steads my foe.

---

5   Then plainly know my heart's dear love is set,
     On the fair daughter of rich Capulet.

6   As mine on hers, so hers is set on mine,
     And all combin'd, save what thou must combine
     By holy marriage.

7   When and where and how
     We met, we woo'd, and made exchange of vow,
     I'll tell thee as we pass, but this I pray,
     That thou consent to marry us to-day.

Romeo

1   {I have not graced my} bed to night {-}
     {†}   the sweeter rest was mine.

---

2   With Rosaline, my ghostly Father ?

3   No,
   I have forgot that name, and that names woe.

---

4   I have beene feasting with mine enemie,
   Where on a sudden one hath wounded me,
   That's by me wounded: both our remedies
   Within thy helpe and holy phisicke lies:
   I beare no hatred, blessed man: for loe
   My intercession likewise steads my foe.

---

5   Then plainly know my hearts deare Love is set,
   On the faire daughter of rich Capulet:
   As mine on hers, so hers is set on mine;
   And all combin'd, save what thou must combine
   By holy marriage: when and where, and how,
   We met, we wooed, and made exchange of vow:
   Ile tell thee as we passe, but this I pray,
   That thou consent to marrie us to day.

• while the unbembellished opening control (F #1-3) is interrupted by facts (the short F #2, 2/0), F #4's explanation of feasting 'with mine enemie' leading to the request for the Frier's 'helpe and holy phisicke' becomes purely emotional (0/5), the last three and a half lines of the request being set as surround phrases

• and then, hardly surprisingly, the confession that he loves Juliet is passionate, (2/2, F #5's opening two lines)

• but what is surprising is that the next three lines explaining that the feelings between he and Juliet are reciprocal and all that now is required is marriage, plus the final line and a half requesting the marriage, is unembellished, thus matching Juliet's careful control when she broached the subject of marriage with him earlier (speech #24 above)

• two lovely extra personal touches can be seen in, first, the two emotional surround phrases formed in part by the semicolon ' : As mine on hers, so hers is set on mine ; /And all combin'd, save what thou must combine/By holy marriage : ', and in the extra breath thoughts as the onrushed 'when and where, and how,/We met . . .' hopefully puts off any possible questions from the Frier, also heightened by being set within another surround phrase

The Tragedie of Romeo and Juliet
Romeo

No matter : Get thee gone,
5.1.32 - 57

Background: instead of the happy news, Romeo's man has brought him seemingly incontrovertible news of Juliet's death: having left Verona before the Frier Lawrence-Juliet potion plot was formed, and since a letter from Lawrence which should have reached Romeo before his man arrived has been unavoidably delayed, Romeo believes the news, and makes plans accordingly

Style: initially to one man, and then solo

Where: a street in Mantua
To Whom: self, and direct audience address

# of Lines: 26

Probable Timing: 1.15 minutes

Take Note: Despite the onrush of F #2, which most modern texts reset as four separate and more rational sentences, there seems to be a great growth in Romeo's ability to control himself, with the speech displaying two very different states of determination, the final sense of icy control markedly different from the opening surround phrase mix.

Romeo

1 No matter, get thee gone,
   And hire those horses; I'll be with thee straight.

2 Well, Juliet, I will lie with thee to night.

3 Lets see for means.

4 O mischief, thou art swift,
   To enter in the thoughts of desperate men!

5 I do remember an apothecary -
   And hereabouts [a] dwells - which late I noted
   In tatt'red weeds, with overwhelming brows,
   Culling of simples, meagre were his looks,
   Sharp misery had worn him to the bones;
   And in his needy shop a tortoise hung,
   An alligator stuff'd, and other skins
   Of ill-shap'd fishes, and about his shelves
   A beggarly account of empty boxes,
   Green earthen pots, bladders, and musty seeds,
   Remnants of packthread, and old cakes of roses
   Were thinly scattered, to make up a show.

6 Noting this penury, to myself I said,
   "An' if a man did need a poison now,
   Whose sale is present death in Mantua,
   Here lives a caitiff wretch would sell it him."

7 O, this same thought did but forerun my need,
   And this same needy man must sell it me.

8 As I remember, this should be the house.

9 Being [holiday], the beggar's shop is shut.

10 What ho, apothecary?

Romeo

1   No matter : Get thee gone,
     And hyre those Horses, Ile be with thee straight.

2   Well Juliet, I will lie with thee to night:
     Lets see for meanes: O mischiefe thou art swift,
     To enter in the thoughts of desperate men:
     I do remember an Appothecarie,
     And here abouts [ ] dwells, which late I noted
     In tattred weeds, with overwhelming browes,
     Culling of Simples, meager were his lookes,
     Sharpe miserie had worne him to the bones:
     And in his needie shop a Tortoyrs hung,
     An Allegater stuft, and other skins
     Of ill shap'd fishes, and about his shelves,
     A beggerly account of emptie boxes,
     Greene earthen pots, Bladders, and mustie seedes,
     Remnants of packthred, and old cakes of Roses
     Were thinly scattered, to make up a shew.

3   Noting this penury, to my selfe I said,
     An if a man did need a poyson now,
     Whose sale is present death in Mantua,
     Here lives a Caitiffe wretch would sell it him.

4   O this same thought did but fore-run my need,
     And this same needie man must sell it me.

5   As I remember, this should be the house,
     Being [holy day], the beggers shop is shut.

6   What ho?

7   Appothecarie?

• Romeo's determination can be seen from the outset, the first five passionate lines (4/3) of coming to terms with the facts and deciding
what to do about them being entirely composed of five surround
phrases, the passion intermingled with three ice-cold unembellished
instructions and determinations, from the opening dismissal of his
servant's concern ' . No matter : ' and 'Ile be with thee straight.', and
the reassuring of his (believed-to-be) dead wife 'I will lie with thee to
night', the last two heightened even further by being monosyllabic

• the recollection and description of the 'Appothecarie' and his 'needie
shop' remain somewhat passionate (6/7, F #2's last twelve lines)

• F #3's recollection of his original thought that here was a 'Caitiffe'
would sell him a 'poyson' even though the punishment for so doing
is 'present death' is also emotional and intellectual (2/3 in just four
lines)

• the finish shows an entirely different form of determination, for the
last five lines (F #4-7) attempting to raise the 'Appothecarie' who
'must sell' him the poison are totally unembellished, suggesting he
either has discovered an amazing sense of self-control or is being quiet in an effort not to draw attention to himself and his potentially
illegal act

The Tragedie of Romeo and Juliet

Paris

Give me thy Torch Boy, hence and stand aloft,
between 5.3.1 - 21

Background: the potion the Frier gave Juliet has worked well, and everyone believes she has died on the morning of her wedding to Paris: Paris has come to mourn at the Capulet monument where her body has been laid to rest: this speech starts the scene, and as such is self-explanatory

Style: as part of a two-handed scene

Where: outside the Capulet monument

To Whom: his Page

# of Lines: 19

Probable Timing: 1.00 minutes

Take Note: The modern texts' thirteen sentences suggest a very rational young man: F's six, especially the onrushed F #1 (usually split into six modern sentences) shows a very disturbed young man, at least at the top of the speech – until he settles into his self prescribed task of nightly worship.

Paris

1 Give me thy torch, boy.

2 Hence and stand [aloof].

3 Yet put it out, for I would not be seen.

4 Under yond [yew] trees lay thee all along,
   Holding thy ear close to the hollow ground,
   So shall no foot upon the churchyard tread,
   Being loose, unfirm, with digging up of graves,
   But thou shalt hear it.

5   Whistle then to me
   As signal that thou [hearst] something approach.

6 Give me those flowers.

7   Do as I bid thee, go.

---

8 Sweet flower, with flowers thy bridal bed I strew -
   O woe, thy canopy is dust and stones ! -
   Which with sweet water nightly I will dew,
   Or wanting that, with tears distill'd by moans.

9 The obsequies that I for thee will keep
   Nightly shall be to strew thy grave and weep.
                    [**Whistle Boy**]

10 The boy gives warning, something doth approach.

11 What cursed foot wanders this [way] to night,
    To cross my obsequies and true love's [rite]?

12 What, with a torch?

13   Muffle me, night, [awhile]

Paris

1   Give me thy Torch Boy, hence and stand [aloft],
    Yet put it out, for I would not be seene:
    Under yond [young] Trees lay thee all along,
    Holdingthy eare close to the hollow ground,
    So shall no foot upon the Churchyard tread,
    Being loose, unfirme with digging up of Graves,
    But thou shalt heare it: whistle then to me,
    As signall that thou [hearest] some thing approach,
    Give me those flowers.

2   Do as I bid thee, go.

---

3   Sweet Flower with flowers thy Bridall bed I strew:
    O woe, thy Canopie is dust and stones,
    Which with sweet water nightly I will dewe,
    Or wanting that, with teares destil'd by mones;
    The obsequies that I for thee will keepe,
    Nightly shall be, to strew thy grave, and weepe.
              [**Whistle Boy**]

4   The Boy gives warning, something doth approach,
    What cursed foot wanders this [wayes] to night,
    To crosse my obsequies, and true loves [right]?

5   What with a Torch?

6   Muffle me night [a while].

• F #1's first line for the boy to leave is factual (2/0), while the further six lines of explanation and instructions become much more emotional (3/5, the next five and a half lines) until the very last (almost, save for 'signall') unembellished instruction that the boy should

> " . . . whistle then to me,/As signall that thou hearest some thing approach,"

the attempted control somewhat undone by the ungrammatical final order, also unembellished of 'Give me those flowers.'

• the first short sentence (F #2) 'Do as I bid thee, go.' is made even more powerful by being both monosyllabic and unembellished, and the only surround phrase that immediately follows it underscores both the "why" and the pain and determination of his purpose ' . Sweet Flower with flowers thy Bridall bed I strew : '

• as he begins to 'strew' the flowers, as with the first sentence, he starts out in control (3/1, F #3's first two lines), but then for the rest of the sentence he becomes emotional (0/4, F #3's last four lines), which spills into the 'Boy' giving 'warning, something doth approach' (1/2, F #4)

• and then his sense of control as seen in speech #11 returns, with two very precise short speeches taking charge of the situation to end the speech, the monosyllabic F #5 (1/0) and the unembellished F #6

The Tragedie of Julius Caesar

Brutus

That you do love me, I am nothing jealous:
1.2.162 - 175

Background: The following is Brutus' careful, but still not yet committed, response to Cassius' anti-Cæsar overtures

Style: as part of a two-handed scene

Where: a street in Rome

To Whom: Cassius

# of Lines: 14

Probable Timing: 0.45 minutes

Take Note: The question of Brutus' honour and how soon he reacts to temptation is the stuff of academic commentary, and F's orthography may be able to add pertinent information. In the shaded section F's opening parenthesis makes it abundantly clear that Brutus is already tempted and might be 'so' 'moov'd' at a later date by this same argument, though not just now - the placing of 'so' outside the bracket being the key: most modern texts set the 'so' inside the bracket, and unfortunately this seems to turn Brutus' reply into a much more morally correct lack of interest in any argument so far presented.

Brutus

1   That you do love me, I am nothing jealous ;
    What you would work me to, I have some aim.

2   How I have thought of this, and of these times,
    I shall recount hereafter.

3   For this present,
    I would not, so with love I might entreat you,
    Be any further mov'd.

4   What you have said,
    I will consider ; what you have to say
    I will with patience hear and find a time
    Both meet to hear and answer such high things.

5   Till then, my noble friend, chew upon this :
    Brutus had rather be a villager
    [Than] to repute himself a son of Rome
    Under these hard conditions as this time
    Is like to lay upon us.

Brutus

1   That you do love me, I am nothing jealous :
    What you would worke me too, I have some ayme:
    How I have thought of this, and of these times
    I shall recount heereafter.

2   For this present,
    I would not so (with love I might intreat you)
    Be any further moov'd: What you have said,
    I will consider: what you have to say
    I will with patience heare, and finde a time
    Both meete to heare, and answer such high things.

3   Till then, my Noble Friend, chew upon this:
    Brutus had rather be a Villager,
    [Then] to repute himselfe a Sonne of Rome
    Under these hard Conditions, as this time
    Is like to lay upon us.

• that Brutus is taking great care in how much he commits to from the outset can be seen not only in F #1 being completely set as (three) surround phrases, but also in the fact that the first line of the first two sentences are unembellished as well

• however, it does seem that his feelings are stirred by the proposition, for F #1 is totally emotional (0/3), and though he seems to re-establish control via F #2's opening calm, following the all-telling surround phrase ' : What you have said,/I will consider : ', F #2's last two and a half lines are also emotional (0/4)

• but when he does finally commit himself, he does so fully, with F #3 opening via the unequivocal surround phrase ' . Till then my Noble Friend, chew upon this : ', the whole of the ensuing self-definition spoken highly intellectually (6/2)

The Tragedie of Julius Caesar

Brutus

It must be by his death: and for my part,
2.1.10 - 34

Background: Cassius has followed up the arguments by sending Brutus several messages in different handwritings purporting to be from different concerned citizens, all urging Brutus to action, leading Brutus to explore the inevitable.

Style: solo

Where: the garden of Brutus' home

To Whom: self, and audience

# of Lines: 25

Probable Timing: 1.15 minutes

Take Note: That Brutus is racking his brains to solve the dilemma of moving against his one time mentor can be seen in the concentrated thought patterns F's surround phrases denote, with F's first four sentences opening with at least one, and the last two sentences ending the same way. (This is a tremendous rarity, with virtually no parallel throughout the canon.)

Brutus

1 It must be by his death ; and for my part,
  I know no personal cause to spurn at him,
  But for the general.

2   He would be crown'd:
  How that might change his nature, there's the question.

3 It is the bright day that brings forth the adder,
  And that craves wary walking.

4   Crown him that,
  And then I grant we put a sting in him
  That at his will he may do danger with.

5 Th'abuse of greatness is when it disjoins
  Remorse from power; and to speak truth of Cæsar,
  I have not known when his affections sway'd
  More [than] his reason.

6   But 'tis a common proof
  That lowliness is young ambition's ladder,
  Whereto the climber-upward turns his face;
  But when he once attains the upmost round,
  He then unto the ladder turns his back,
  Looks in the clouds, scorning the base degrees
  By which he did ascend.

7   So Cæsar may ;
  Then lest he may, prevent.

8   And since the quarrel
  Will bear no color for the thing he is,
  Fashion it thus: that what he is, augmented,
  Would run to these and these extremities;
  And therefore think him as a serpent's egg,
  Which, hatch'd, would as his kind grow mischievous,
  And kill him in the shell !

Brutus

1   It must be by his death : and for my part,
I know no personall cause, to spurne at him,
But for the generall.

2   He would be crown'd:
How that might change his nature, there's the question?

3   It is the bright day, that brings forth the Adder,
And that craves warie walking: Crowne him that,
And then I graunt we put a Sting in him,
That at his will he may doe danger with.

4   Th'abuse of Greatnesse, is, when it dis-joynes
Remorse from Power: And to speake truth of Cæsar,
I have not knowne, when his Affections sway'd
More [then] his Reason.

5   But 'tis a common proofe,
That Lowlynesse is young Ambitions Ladder,
Whereto the Climber upward turnes his Face:
But when he once attaines the upmost Round,
He then unto the Ladder turnes his Backe,
Lookes in the Clouds, scorning the base degrees
By which he did ascend: so Cæsar may;
Then least he may, prevent.

6   And since the Quarrell
Will beare no colour, for the thing he is,
Fashion it thus; that what he is, augmented,
Would runne to these, and these extremities:
And therefore thinke him as a Serpents egge,
Which hatch'd, would as his kinde grow mischievous;
And kill him in the shell.

• the unequivocal opening ' . It must be by his death : ' couldn't be any bleaker, expressed as it is via a monosyllabic unembellished surround phrase, and it seems the inevitability of Cæsar's death has an emotional effect on him for the rest of F #1 (0/3)

• the same kind of bleak unembellished surround phrase realisation opens F #2, only the key words 'nature' and 'question' breaking the monosyllabic pattern "He would be crown'd:/How that might change his nature, there's the question ? "

• amazingly, F #3 starts the same way, with just one key word, 'Adder', breaking the line's monosyllabic and unembellished pattern. "It is the bright day, that brings forth the Adder,/And that craves warie walking : "

• but the opening of F#4 " . Th'abuse of Greatnesse, is, when it dis-joynes/Remorse from Power :" though still surround-phrase height-ened, now shows more release and becomes polysyllabic as more abstract fears are explored: indeed, in equating Cæsar as the 'Adder' and expanding on the dangerous 'Sting' Cæsar could now execute – though he has never yet let 'his Affections' sway his 'Reason' - Brutus' argument becomes highly passionate (8/7 in just seven lines to the end of F #4), as if he cannot prevent his thoughts from bursting forth

• yet as he finally establishes his 'common proofe' focusing on 'Ambitions Ladder' he becomes intellectual (5/1, F #5's first two and a half lines), only turning passionate with the corollary that the higher one climbs the more likely one is to turn his back on those below (4/4 the next three and a half lines), leading him to the firm surround phrase un-derstanding of what might happen to Cæsar, and what he, Brutus must do about it ": so Cæsar may ; /Then least he may, prevent . "

• which leads to great emotion (2/6, F #7) as Brutus realises what action he must take ' ; And kill him in the shell . ', the surround phrase strength of the conclusion supported by the other, in part emotional, surround phrase in the sentence, thus stressing the only reason by which Cæsar's death can be justified, viz. ' ; that what he is, augment-ed,/Would runne to these, and these extremities :)'

The Tragedie of Julius Caesar

Antony

O mighty Cæsar ! Dost thou lye so lowe?
3.1.148 - 163

Background: Promised that he can meet the conspirators and 'Depart untouch'd', Antony has arrived at the Senate. Despite Brutus' greeting of 'Welcome Mark Antony', his first words are to Cæsar's freshly stabbed corpse, and only then to the conspirators.

Style: mixed address

Where: the Senate

To Whom: initially to the dead Cæsar, and then to the conspirators

# of Lines: 16

Probable Timing: 0.50 minutes

Take Note: The shorter F sentences opening and closing the speech suggest that Antony is working very hard to maintain control and to not let his thoughts or emotions run away with him. However, the fact that the first four sentences, three of which are five words or less, all show a different pattern suggesting that he is in difficulty from the outset.

Antony

1   O mighty Cæsar ! dost thou lie so low?

2   Are all thy conquests, glories, triumphs, spoils,
     Shrunk to this little measure?

3   Fare thee well !

4   I know not, gentlemen, what you intend,
     Who else must be let blood, who else is rank;
     If I myself, there is no hour so fit
     As Cæsar's death's hour, nor no instrument
     Of half that worth as those your swords, made rich
     With the most noble blood of all this world.

5   I do beseech ye, if you bear me hard,
     Now, whil'st your purpled hands do reek and smoke,
     Fulfill your pleasure.

6   Live a thousand years,
     I shall not find myself so apt to die,
     No place will please me so, no mean of death,
     As here by Cæsar, and by you cut off,
     The choice and master spirits of this age.

Antony

1   O mighty Cæsar !

2   Dost thou lye so lowe?

3   Are all thy Conquests, Glories, Triumphes, Spoiles,
    Shrunke to this little Measure?

4   Fare thee well.

5   I know not Gentlemen what you intend,
    Who else must be let blood, who else is ranke:
    If I my selfe, there is no houre so fit
    As Cæsars deaths houre; nor no Instrument
    Of halfe that worth, as those your Swords; made rich
    With the most Noble blood of all this World.

6   I do beseech yee, if you beare me hard,
    Now, whil'st your purpled hands do reeke and smoake,
    Fulfill your pleasure.

7   Live a thousand yeeres,
    I shall not finde my selfe so apt to dye.

8   No place will please me so, no meane of death,
    As heere by Cæsar, and by you cut off,
    The Choice and Master Spirits of this Age.

• the varying flood of thoughts shows no consistency, with the acknowl-
edgement of Cæsar's body being purely factual (F #1, 1/0); the realisation that Cæsar is no longer triumphant emotional (F #2, 0/2); the
supposition that death has shrunk all of Cæsar's glories passionate (F
#3, 5/3); and then F #4's first 'farewell' is totally unembellished

• and after a careful intellectually/emotionally held-in-check skirting
of 'who else is ranke' (1/1, the first two lines of F #5), Antony finally
succumbs to emotion as he voices that if he is to die, now is the best
time (5/13, the next nine lines, from F #5's last four lines through to
the opening line of F #8)

• and as he gets to the crux of his request (F #5), so the only surround
phrases of the speech appear " : If I my selfe, there is no houre so fit/
As Cæsars deaths houre; nor no Instrument/Of halfe that worth, as
those your Swords; made rich/With the most Noble blood of all this
World . " the emotion even further heightened by all three phrases
being linked by the only emotional semicolons in the speech

• yet at the very last minute Antony manages to regain superb intellectual (ironic?) control, in his last line 'praise' of the conspirators as
'The Choice and Master Spirits of this Age.' (4/0)

The Tragedie of Julius Caesar

Antony

O pardon me, thou bleeding peece of Earth:
3.1.254 - 275

Background: Left alone with the body, Antony is at last free to give vent to his true feelings.

Style: solo

Where: the Senate

To Whom: to the dead body, self and audience

# of Lines: 22

Probable Timing: 1.10 minutes

Take Note: Though the sentence structure of the two texts is identical, the addition of exclamation marks by most modern texts make Antony's growth towards his vow more predictable and far more vehement than F #1-3 suggest.

Antony

1 O pardon me, thou bleeding piece of earth :
  That I am meek and gentle with these butchers!

2 Thou art the ruins of the noblest man
  That ever lived in the tide of times.

3 Woe to the hand that shed this costly blood !

4 Over thy wounds now do I prophesy,
  (Which like dumb mouths do ope their ruby lips,
  To beg the voice and utterance of my tongue)
  A curse shall light upon the limbs of men;
  Domestic fury and fierce civil strife
  Shall cumber all the parts of Italy;
  Blood and destruction shall be so in use,
  And dreadful objects so familiar,
  That mothers shall but smile when they behold
  Their infants quartered with the hands of war;
  All pity chok'd with custom of fell deeds,
  And Cæsar's spirit, ranging for revenge,
  With Ate by his side come hot from hell,
  Shall in these confines with a monarch's voice
  Cry "Havoc ! " and let slip the dogs of war,
  That this foul deed, shall smell above the earth
  With carrion men, groaning for burial.

Antony

1　O pardon me, thou bleeding peece of Earth :
　That I am meeke and gentle with these Butchers.

2　Thou art the Ruines of the Noblest man
　That ever lived in the Tide of Times.

3　Woe to the hand that shed this costly Blood.

4　Over thy wounds, now do I Prophesie,
　(Which like dumbe mouthes do ope their Ruby lips,
　To begge the voyce and utterance of my Tongue)
　A Curse shall light upon the limbes of men;
　Domesticke Fury, and fierce Civill strife,
　Shall cumber all the parts of Italy :
　Blood and destruction shall be so in use,
　And dreadfull Objects so familiar,
　That Mothers shall but smile, when they behold
　Their Infants quartered with the hands of Warre :
　All pitty choak'd with custome of fell deeds,
　And Cæsars Spirit ranging for Revenge,
　With Ate by his side, come hot from Hell,
　Shall in these Confines, with a Monarkes voyce,
　Cry havocke, and let slip the Dogges of Warre,
　That this foule deede, shall smell above the earth
　With Carrion men, groaning for Buriall.

- though Antony's first address, now at last alone, to his dead mentor opens passionately (F #1, 2/2) and is formed by the only surround phrases in the speech, it is not followed up by a sentence ending exclamation mark, the lack suggesting Antony's initial outburst may be over

- indeed it seems that Antony gains self-control both in the praise for dead Cæsar as well as in the first swearing against 'the hand that shed this costly Blood' (5/1, F #2-3): the whole is deadly for its intellectual ferocity, especially when compared to what most modern texts suggest - for once again this section does not end with an emotional releasing exclamation mark as in most modern texts

- not surprisingly, the sight of Cæsar's wounds, with his description of them as 'dumbe mouthes', and the start of his 'Curse' release Antony's passion (4/5, F #4's first four lines), which is sustained (3/2 in the two lines between the semicolon and the next colon) as he springs, via the only semicolon in the speech, to prophesying the two things that would terrify an Elizabethan audience, 'Domesticke Fury, and fierce Civill strife'

- the impact of this is not lost on him, for the first of at least six extra breath thoughts make their first appearance, suggesting that he needs the extra breaths to handle the frightening thoughts of what is to come, followed by the only unembellished line in the section, 'Blood and destruction shall be so in use,', unequivocally spelling out the inevitable result, but so quietly in comparison to what surrounds it, it seems as if Antony has difficulty in just saying the words

- and the remainder of the onrushed sentence now struggles between the polar opposites of intellect and emotion, with the horrific images of 'Mothers' smiling at their slaughtered children handled intellectually (4/2); the neutering of pity, emotionally (0/3 in just one line); 'Cæsar's Spirit ranging for Revenge', intellectually (7/2 in three lines); and the final cry of 'havocke' and letting 'slip the Dogges of Warre', passionately emotional (4/6, F #3's last three lines)

The Tragedie of Julius Caesar

Antony

This is a slight unmeritable man,
between 4.1.12 - 40

Background: The following occurs following the first on-stage meeting of the tripartite leadership (established to restore order and defeat the conspirators). With Lepidus having left, Antony is exceedingly candid with Octavius about his feelings for their partner.

Style: as part of a two handed scene

Where: unspecified, a meeting room at the Senate

To Whom: Octavius

# of Lines: 26

Probable Timing: 1.15 minutes

Take Note: At first it seems that Antony's dislike of Lepidus can be held in check, for though F #1 opens with a surround phrase, unembellished till the very last scornful dismissive image, the sentence is only mildly intellectual (2/0 in four lines), but then F's orthography shows how disturbed Antony becomes (with a man unworthy to stand within Cæsar's shadow perhaps) before he manages to re-establish control.

Antony

1   This is a slight unmeritable man,
    Meet to be sent on errands; is it fit,
    The three-fold world divided, he should stand
    One of the three to share it?

2   And though we lay these honors on this man
    To ease our selves of divers sland'rous loads,
    He shall but bear them as the ass bears gold,
    To groan and sweat under the business,
    Either led or driven, as we point the way;
    And having brought our treasure where we will,
    Then take we down his load, and turn him off
    (Like to the empty ass) to shake his ears
    And graze in commons.

3   {†}{You say he is} a tried, and valiant soldier.

4   So is my horse, Octavius, and for that
    I do appoint him store of provender.

5   It is a creature that I teach to fight,
    To wind, to stop, to run directly on,
    His corporal motion govern'd by my spirit;
    And in some taste is Lepidus but so:
    He must be taught, and train'd, and bid go forth;
    A barren-spirited fellow; one that feeds
    On objects, arts and imitations,
    Which, out of use, and stal'd by other men,
    Begin his fashion.

6   Do not talk of him
    But as a property.

Antony

1   This is a slight unmeritable man,
     Meet to be sent on Errands: is it fit
     The three-fold World divided, he should stand
     One of the three to share it?

---

2   And though we lay these Honours on this man,
     To ease our selves of divers sland'rous loads,
     He shall but beare them, as the Asse beares Gold,
     To groane and swet under the Businesse,
     Either led or driven, as we point the way :
     And having brought our Treasure, where we will,
     Then take we downe his Load, and turne him off
     (Like to the empty Asse) to shake his eares,
     And graze in Commons.

---

3 {†}{You say hee is} a tried, and valiant Souldier .

4   So is my Horse Octavius, and for that
     I do appoint him store of Provender.

5   It is a Creature that I teach to fight,
     To winde, to stop, to run directly on:
     His corporall Motion, govern'd by my Spirit,
     And in some taste, is Lepidus but so:
     He must be taught, and train'd, and bid go forth:
     A barren spirited Fellow; one that feeds
     On Objects, Arts and Imitations.

6   Which out of use, and stal'de by other men
     Begin his fashion.

7   Do not talke of him,
     But as a property.

• on the one hand the unembellished phrases suggest that Antony can deny without too much problem Lepidus' worthiness to share in the 'three-fold World'

> "is it fit/ . . . he should stand/One of the three to share it?"

he being only fit to be

> "Either led or driven, as we point the way"

> "To ease our selves of divers sland'rous loads"

> "He must be taught, and train'd, and bid go forth"

• yet F #2's images dismissing Lepidus as an 'Asse' are scathing, and not only are they passionate (8/10) but four of at least six extra breath-thoughts scattered through the speech make their appearance here, suggesting either that Antony is trying to rein himself in and needs the extra breaths to do so, or, the exact opposite, that he is being over-ly-abusive in making the most of even the tiniest points of ridicule

• F #3's challenge to Octavius as to Lepidus' reputation is the final mo-ment of passion (1/2), its shortness suggesting a last attack before es-tablishing self-control

• and even though the dismissive comparisons continue, Antony dwell-ing at length on comparing Lepidus to a horse that needs training, his intellect takes over (11/2, the nine lines of F #4-5), and the scorn is emphasised by the surround phrases ending F #5

> " : He must be taught, and train'd, and bid go forth : /A bar-ren spirited Fellow ; one that feeds/On Objects, Arts and Imitations ."

a scorn even further heightened by the fact that the surround phrases are preceded by two more of the extra breath-thoughts and linked by the only emotional semicolon in the speech

• and the ending of the speech is not only emotional (0/2, F #6-7) it is also ungrammatical, with most modern texts adding the non-syntac-tical F #6 to the previous sentence: as set it seems that Antony most definitely needs a pause (however ungrammatical) before continuing

The Tragedie of Julius Caesar

Brutus

You wrong'd your selfe to write in such a case.
between 4.3.6 - 28

Background: In his funeral oration Antony has succeeded in turning the crowd against the conspirators who have fled from Rome.
Octavius, Cæsar's nephew, has been welcomed into Rome, and a
tripartite leadership agreement to restore order and defeat the conspirators has been arranged between himself and the insignificant
Lepidus (see previous speech). In the mean time the conspirators
are attempting to levy support, money, and men to withstand the
inevitable tripartite-led war against them. In so doing Cassius is
prepared to support his men who cut corners to get what they want,
including one Lucius Pella accused of bribery, even writing letters
of support on their behalf, which leads 'honourable' Brutus to
speak as follows.

Style: as part of a two-handed scene

Where: Brutus' battlefield tent

To Whom: Cassius

# of Lines: 18

Probable Timing: 0.55 minutes

Take Note: F's orthography shows how well Brutus is able to control
his emotions and stay highly factually/intellectual focused in his
'Chasticement' of Cassius, almost until the end of the speech.

Brutus

1   You wrong'd yourself to write in such a case .

2   Let me tell you, Cassius, you yourself
     Are much condemn'd to have an itching palm,
     To sell and mart your offices for gold
     To undeservers.

3   The name of Cassius honors this corruption,
     And chastisement doth therefore hide his head.

4   Remember March, the ides of March remember :
     Did not great Julius bleed for justice' sake?

5   What villain touch'd his body, that did stab
     And not for justice?

6   What? shall one of us,
     That struck the foremost man of all this world
     But for supporting robbers, shall we now
     Contaminate our fingers with base bribes?
     And sell the mighty space of our large honors
     For so much trash as may be grasped thus?

7   I had rather be a dog, and bay the moon,
     [Than] such a Roman.

Brutus

1   You wrong'd your selfe to write in such a case .

---

2   Let me tell you Cassius, you your selfe
     Are much condemn'd to have an itching Palme,
     To sell, and Mart your Offices for Gold
     To Undeservers.

---

3   The name of Cassius Honors this corruption,
     And Chasticement doth therefore hide his head.

---

4   Remember March, the Ides of March remember :
     Did not great Julius bleede for Justice sake?

5   What Villaine touch'd his body, that did stab,
     And not for Justice?

6   What?

7   Shall one of Us,
     That strucke the Formost man of all this World,
     But for supporting Robbers: shall we now,
     Contaminate our fingers, with base Bribes?
     And sell the mighty space of our large Honors
     For so much trash, as may be grasped thus?

8   I had rather be a Dogge, and bay the Moone,
     [Then] such a Roman.

- the fact that there are no surround phrases and just one piece of major punctuation suggests that this highly intellectual speech (until the last sentence) comes springing forth without premeditation, making its lack of emotional release even more remarkable

- with such a springing forth, the lack of released emotion (22/6 the first sixteen lines of the speech) provides great witness to how much Btutus wishes to let the facts speak for themselves rather than let his heart do the work for him

- however, the sudden passion of the final sentence (F #8, 3/2) suggests just how much of a strain this causes him, especially since the out-burst has been preceded by three extra breath-thoughts that appear in the middle of F #7 as the appalling thought of 'shall we now/ Contaminate our fingers, with base Bribes', thus undoing all the hopes of speech #6 above, is voiced: the extra breaths suggest that Brutus is either taking great care to get the final points across and/or is almost speechless at the points he must now utter

- that the speech opens with a short, one line, monosyllabic sentence shows with what a tight rein Brutus is holding himself in check

- the few occasions of emotion that do break through deal in concepts of honour and its besmirching, with the moment of Cæsar's death, 'Did not great Julius bleede for Justice sake' being matched against the rumours of Cassius accepting bribes 'your selfe/Are much con-demn'd to have an itching Palme' and against any 'Villaine' that touch'd Cæsar's body for anything other than 'Justice'

The Tragedie of Hamlet, Prince of Denmarke

Hamlet

Angels and Ministers of Grace defend us:
1.4.39 - 57

Background: Faring no better than the soldiers in questioning the Ghost, Horatio has brought Hamlet to the battlements to see what effect his presence might have.

Style: one on one as part of a four-handed scene

Where: on the battlements of Elsinore castle

To Whom: the Ghost, in front of Horatio and the soldier Marcellus

# of Lines: 19

Probable Timing: 1.00 minutes

Take Note: Hamlet's strength of mind and purpose can be seen in that despite facing an apparition he still is able to maintain solid intellectual discipline, at least for the first two sentences of the speech (16/6, F #1-2) - and even in the last feverish questioning his passions rather than rampant emotions take over (6/9, F #3).

Hamlet

1   Angels and ministers of grace defend us!

2   Be thou a spirit of health, or goblin damn'd,
    Bring with thee airs from heaven, or blasts from hell,
    Be thy [intents] wicked, or charitable,
    Thou com'st in such a questionable shape
    That I will speak to thee.

3   I'll call thee Hamlet,
    King, father, royal Dane.

4   Oh, [ ], answer me !

5   Let me not burst in ignorance, but tell
    Why thy canoniz'd bones hearsed in death,
    Have burst their cerements; why the sepulchre,
    Wherein we saw thee quietly [interr'd],
    Hath op'd his ponderous and marble jaws
    To cast thee up again .

6   What may this mean,
    That thou, dead corse, again in complete steel
    Revisits thus the glimpses of the moon,
    Making night hideous,   and we fools of nature
    So horridly to shake our disposition
    With thoughts beyond [the] reaches of our souls?

7   Say why is this ?wherefore ?what should we do ?

Hamlet

1   Angels and Ministers of Grace defend us :
Be thou a Spirit of health, or Goblin damn'd,
Bring with thee ayres from Heaven, or blasts from Hell,
Be thy [events] wicked or charitable,
Thou com'st in such a questionable shape
That I will speake to thee.

2   Ile call thee Hamlet,
King, Father, Royall Dane :   Oh, [oh], answer me,
Let me not burst in Ignorance; but tell
Why thy Canoniz'd bones Hearsed in death,
Have burst their cerments, why the Sepulcher
Wherein we saw thee quietly [enurn'd],
Hath op'd his ponderous and Marble jawes,
To cast thee up againe?

3   What may this meane?
That thou dead Coarse againe in compleat steele,
Revisits thus the glimpses of the Moone,
Making Night hidious? And we fooles of Nature
So horridly to shake our disposition,
With thoughts beyond [thee;] reaches of our Soules,
Say, why is this? wherefore? what should we doe?

- considering the potential fear shown by others who have faced it, his steadfastness and courage is even more remarkable, as shown in the quiet of the calm unembellished lines, not only when challenging the Ghost

  "Be thy events wicked or charitable,/Thou com'st in such a questionable shape"

  but also realising the possible results of any intercourse with it

  "So horridly to shake our disposition/With thoughts beyond thee"

  and especially when demanding point blank an explanation

  "Say, why is this? wherefore?"

- the few surround phrases define the key moments of Hamlet's struggle, from the opening ' . Angels and Ministers of Grace defend us : ' through to

  " . Ile call thee Hamlet,/King, Father, Royall Dane : Oh, [oh], answer me,/Let me not burst in Ignorance ; "

  and the highly disturbed broken off questioning any basic belief which

  " ; reaches of our Soules,/Say, why is this ? wherefore ? what should we doe ? "

- the only moment emotion breaks through is at the top of F #3 as he repeats his demand that the Ghost tell him 'What may this meane?' (1/5, F #3's first one and half lines), though this quickly turns to intellectual passion once the specifics of time and place are stated (5/3 the next four lines)

- and then he reveals his strength once again, for the final line reiterating his demand for information is almost completely calm and unembellished (0/1)

The Tragedie of Hamlet, Prince of Denmarke

Hamlet

Oh all you host of Heaven! Oh Earth; what els?

1.5.92 - 112

Background: The Ghost has left, leaving Hamlet alone for the second time in the play.

Style: solo

Where: on the battlements of Elsinore castle

To Whom: self, and direct audience address

# of Lines: 20

Probable Timing: 1.00 minutes

Take Note: The impact of the scene creates a gigantic brainstorm within Hamlet, and F's orthography shows where, how, and why, for within the twenty passionate lines of the speech (28/23 overall) there are eighteen surround phrases, six (logical) colons, ten (emotional) semicolons, and two rare (for an Elizabethan/early Jacobean text) exclamation marks.

Hamlet

1   O all you host of heaven !

2   O earth !

3   What else !

4   And shall I couple hell ?

5   O fie, hold, [hold,] my heart,
     And you, my sinews, grow not instant old,
     But bear me stiffly up.

6   Remember thee !

7   [Ay], thou poor ghost, [whiles] memory holds a seat
     In this distracted globe.

8   Remember thee !

9   Yea, from the table of my memory
     I'll wipe away all trivial fond records,
     All saws of books, all forms, all pressures past
     That youth and observation copied there,
     And thy commandment all alone shall live
     Within the book and volume of my brain,
     Unmix'd with baser matter.

10   Yes, [ ] by heaven !

11   O most pernicious woman !

12   O villain, villain, smiling, damned villain !

13   My tables - [ ] ;meet it is I set it down
     That one may smile, and smile, and be a villain !

14   At least I'm sure it may be so in Denmark.

15   So uncle there you are .

16   Now to my word :
     It is, "Adieu, adieu ! remember me."

17   I have sworn't .

Hamlet

1   Oh all you host of Heaven !

2   Oh Earth ; what els ?

3   And shall I couple Hell ?

4   Oh fie : hold [ ] my heart ;
    And you my sinnewes, grow not instant Old;
    But beare me stiffely up :   Remember thee?

5   [I], thou poore Ghost, [while] memory holds a seate
    In this distracted Globe :   Remember thee?

6   Yea, from the Table of my Memory,
    Ile wipe away all triviall fond Records,
    All sawes of Bookes, all formes, all presures past,
    That youth and observation coppied there;
    And thy Commandment all alone shall live
    Within the Booke and Volume of my Braine,
    Unmixt with baser matter;   yes, [yes], by Heaven:
    Oh most pernicious woman !

7   Oh Villaine, Villaine, smiling damned Villaine !

8   My Tables, my Tables;   meet it is I set it downe,
    That one may smile, and smile and be a Villaine;
    At least I'm sure it may be so in Denmarke;
    So Unckle there you are: now to my word;
    It is;   Adue, Adue, Remember me: I have sworn't.

• the three moments of mental clarity, where intellect dominates and he manages to gain some small measure of self-control, are those where Hamlet assures the departed Ghost that he will be remembered, F #5 (3/2); that his 'Commandment all alone shall live/Within the Booke and Volume of my Braine . . .' (5/2); and the last line of the speech ending with 'I have sworn't' ((3/0), heightened by being only one of two very short unembellished monosyllabic surround phrases in the speech – after all the passion let loose throughout the speech, finally no more need be said

• until the end of the speech nearly all of the semicoloned surround phrases reflect his almost losing himself in the shock of what he has just learned, viz. F #2's " . Oh Earth ; what els ? ", F #4's " hold my heart ; /And you my sinnewes, grow not instant Old ; /But beare me stiffly up : ", and F #6's " ; yes, yes, by Heaven : "

• the most released moment in the speech is the double condemnation of both his mother ('most pernicious woman!') and Claudius (the thrice repeated 'Villaine') – /4 in just ten words, the end of F #6 and the short F #7

• then, as he tries to find a concrete way of setting down all the Ghost has told him, all mental control seems to disappear, for F sets the vastly onrushed and totally ungrammatical #8 (split into five rational sentences by most modern texts, thus diminishing the moment when Hamlet finally breaks), the whole formed by seven consecutive surround phrases shifting rapidly between the need for a permanent record of how ('My Tables'); the sidebar explanations as to why, especially in Denmark; the final knowledge of his Unckle's hand in his father's death; Hamlet's promise to keep his word; the farewell to the Ghost; and the swearing to action

• and this final sentence is marked by the first four lines of passion (5/4) suddenly turning to a final line of intellectual farewell and icy resolve to action, all set with seven pieces of heavy punctuation, five of which are semicolons – a veritable brainstorm indeed

The Tragedie of Hamlet, Prince of Denmarke
Hamlet

Now might I do it pat, now he is praying,
3.2.73 - 96

Background: Hamlet comes across Claudius as Claudius attempts to pray - unattended, defenceless, and vulnerable. This seems a wonderful moment to take revenge - or is it?

Style: solo

Where: a small alcove somewhere off the lobby of the castle

To Whom: self and audience, so that the praying Claudius does not hear

# of Lines: 22

Probable Timing: 1.10 minutes

Take Note: Though most modern texts show a rational Hamlet at the start only becoming more disturbed by the end of the speech as he decides not to kill Claudius at this particular moment, F's Hamlet is nowhere near as controlled as the onrushed F #1 and #3 show (each split into three by most modern texts).

Hamlet

1 Now might I do it pat, now [a] is [a-praying] ;
And now I'll do't.

2   And so [a] goes to heaven,
And so am I reveng'd.

3   That would be scann'd :
A villain kills my father, and for that
I, his [sole] son, do this same villain send
To heaven.

4 [Why], this is hire and salary, not revenge .

5 ['A] took my father grossly, full of bread,
With all his crimes broad blown, as [flush] as May,
And how his audit stands who knows save heaven ?

6 But in our circumstance and course of thought
'Tis heavy with him.

7   And am I then reveng'd,
To take him in the purging of his soul,
When he is fit and season'd for his passage?

8 No !

9 Up, sword, and know thou a more horrid hent :
When he is drunk asleep : or in his rage,
Or in th'incestuous pleasure of his bed,
At gaming, [a-swearing], or about some act
That has no relish of salvation in't -
Then trip him, that his heels may kick at heaven,
And that his soul may be as damn'd and black
As hell, whereto it goes.

10   My mother stays,
This physic but prolongs thy sickly days

Hamlet

1 Now might I do it pat, now [he] is [praying],
   And now Ile doo't, and so he goes to Heaven,
   And so am I reveng'd: that would be scann'd,
   A Villaine killes my Father, and for that
   I his [soule] Sonne, do this same Villaine send
   To heaven.

2   [Oh] this is hyre and Sallery, not Revenge.

3 [He] tooke my Father grossely, full of bread,
   With all his Crimes broad blowne, as [fresh] as May,
   And how his Audit stands, who knowes, save Heaven:
   But in our circumstance and course of thought
   'Tis heavie with him: and am I then reveng'd,
   To take him in the purging of his Soule,
   When he is fit and season'd for his passage?

4   No.

5 Up Sword, and know thou a more horrid hent
   When he is drunke asleepe: or in his Rage,
   Or in th'incestuous pleasure of his bed,
   At gaming, [swearing], or about some acte
   That ha's no rellish of Salvation in't,
   Then trip him, that his heeles may kicke at Heaven,
   And that his Soule may be as damn'd and blacke
   As Hell, whereto it goes.

6   My Mother stayes,
   This Physicke but prolongs thy sickly dayes.

- throughout, the quiet of the unembellished lines points to the dilemma of Hamlet killing a man at prayer, from the opening

> "Now might I do it pat, now [he] is [praying],/ . . . /And so am I reveng'd : that would be scann'd,"

- the remaining quiet lines serve to deepen Hamlet's dilemma, for Claudius, if killed when at prayer, would be in a state of grace, something not granted to Hamlet's father: therefore (in the following the first 'him' refers to his father, the second to Claudius)

> "But in our circumstance and course of thought/'Tis heavie with him : and am I then reveng'd,/To take him . . . /When he is fit and season'd for his passage?"

so Hamlet has no other choice but to accept that his 'Sword' must wait

- the opening onrushed recognition of the dilemma is a mixture of the very quiet (fear of being overheard perhaps?) and passion (5/5, F #1), while the dismissal of such a killing as 'Sallery, not Revenge' becomes a sudden very passionate release (2/2 in just the eight words of the short F #2)

- the onrushed recognition that Claudius killed his father 'With all his Crimes broad blowne' continues the passion (5/4, F #3's first three lines), and then the implications of taking Claudius when saved, as it were, is quiet and circumspect (3/3 from F #3's last four lines through the first three and a half lines of F #5)

- then, for the only time in the speech, Hamlet's emotions begin to colour his envisaging taking Claudius in an act 'That ha's no rellish of Salvation in't' (4/6, F #5's last four lines)

- finally, in resolving to leave Claudius till later and go face his mother, Hamlet's passions return once more (2/3, F #6's line and half)

The Tragedie of Hamlet, Prince of Denmarke

Laertes

I am justly kill'd with mine owne Treacherie.

between 5.2.307 - 331

Background: In the supposed exhibition-only duel at the end of the play Laertes, at the urgings of Claudius, has prepared his unbarbed foil with poison. Claudius has further poisoned a loving-cup, planning that if Hamlet isn't scratched by Laertes' foil at least he will drink the poison. But everything goes awry, with Gertrude drinking the poison, and though Hamlet is fatally scratched, in the ensuing scuffle his and Laertes foils are switched and Laertes is mortally wounded too. The following is Laertes' dying confession.

Style: one on one in front of, and for the benefit of, a larger group

Where: the great hall of the palace

To Whom: Hamlet, in front of Claudius, the dead Gertrude, Horatio, Osricke, with 'lords' and 'other attendants'

# of Lines: 12

Probable Timing: 0.40 minutes

Take Note: While most modern texts allow Laertes a dignified and rational final confession by setting the speech as ten sentences, F's five onrushed sentences and over-punctuated orthography in F #3-4 shows a character much more under the influence of the poison (painfully? struggling to fight the effects?) as well as his urgency to ensure Hamlet understands and forgives all before both of them die.

Laertes

1   I am justly kill'd with mine own treachery .

2   Hamlet, thou art slain .

3   No med'cine in the world can do thee good;
    In thee there is not half an [hour's] life.

4   The treacherous instrument is in thy hand,
    Unbated and envenom'd.

5   The foul practice
    Hath turn'd itself on me.

6   Lo here I lie,
    Never to rise again.

7   Thy mother's poison'd.

8   I can no more - the King, the King's to blame.

9   Exchange forgiveness with me, noble Hamlet .

10 Mine and my father's death come not upon thee,
    Nor thine on me !

Laertes

1　I am justly kill'd with mine owne Treacherie .

2　Hamlet, thou art slaine,
　　No Medicine in the world can do thee good.

3　In thee, there is not halfe an [houre of] life;
　　The Treacherous Instrument is in thy hand,
　　Unbated and envenom'd :　the foule practise:
　　Hath turn'd it selfe on me.

4　　　　　　　　　　　　Loe, heere I lye,
　　Never to rise againe :　Thy Mothers poyson'd:
　　I can no more, the King, the King's too blame.

5　Exchange forgivenesse with me, Noble Hamlet ;
　　Mine and my Fathers death come not upon thee,
　　Nor thine on me.

- of the nine consecutive surround phrases from F #3 to the end of the speech,

  - a/ the first seven of F #3-4 show first the strain and importance to Laertes in explaining all the facts hitherto unknown to Hamlet

  - b/ while the final two (F #5) encompass Laertes' request for Hamlet's forgiveness for Laertes' part in his death, and Laertes' act of forgiveness for Hamlet's part in the deaths of his father and sister, Polonius and Ophelia

- that the structure of F #2 and the opening of F #3 are very different from those of most modern texts have important human implications: again the modern texts seem to concentrate on rationality, while F seems more concerned with Hamlet's (and thus Laertes') fate

  - a/ the onrush of F #2 suggests the emphasis is to be on the fact there is no possible remedy for Hamlet, whereas most modern texts place equal (and more rational) weight on both being 'slain' and 'No med'cine'

  - b/ F's next sentence, F#3, opens with the inescapable fact that for Hamlet 'In thee, there is not half an houre of life;', enhanced by the semicolon ending the surround phrase, whereas in the modern texts this is folded into mt. #3's lack of 'med'cine', with the next new sentence (mt. #4) placing emphasis on 'The treacherous instrument'

- the speech opens passionately (2/3, F #1-2); the circumstances of Hamlet's imminent death are emotional (2/4, the onrushed F #3); the presentation of Laertes' own death (perhaps as proof of his own honesty) and the blaming of Claudius for the Queene's death is passionate (4/6, the onrushed F #4)

- and the dignity that modern texts seem to need throughout the speech is finally shown in the final F moment, where the request for mutual acts of forgiveness are offered intellectually (3/1, the slightly onrushed F #5) – a lovely suggestion of Laertes achieving self control at the last moment

The Tragedie of Troylus and Cressida
Troylus

Oh Pandarus! I tell thee Pandarus;
1.1.48 - 63

Background: the young soldier Troylus is head over heels in love with Cressida, so much so he is almost prepared not to join in the daily battle with the Greeks; to make matters worse, he is getting little sympathy from her uncle Pandarus

Style: as part of a two-handed scene

Where: somewhere in Troy close to the gates and the battle

To Whom: Pandarus

# of Lines: 16

Probable Timing: 0.50 minutes

Take Note: While Troylus' words of love are more than sufficient indication of the depth of his passion, F's more broken up text, both in the extra sentences F #3-6 (set as one long onrush by most modern texts) and in the ungrammatical punctuation towards the end of F #4 shows how both the thoughts and the expression of his love are somewhat less than rational.

Troylus

1   O Pandarus !

2   I tell thee, Pandarus -
When I do tell thee there my hopes lie drown'd,
Reply not in how many fathoms deep
They lie indrench'd.

3   I tell thee I am mad
In Cressid's love; thou answer'st she is fair,
Pourest in the open ulcer of my heart
Her eyes, her hair, her cheek, her [gait], her voice;
Handlest in thy discourse, O, that her hand,
In whose comparison all whites are ink
Writing their own reproach; to whose soft seizure
The cygnet's down is harsh, and spirit of sense
Hard as the palm of ploughman: this thou tell'st me,
As true thou tell'st me, when I say I love her,
But saying thus, instead of oil and balm,
Thou lay'st in every gash that love hath given me
The knife that made it.

Troylus

1   Oh Pandarus !

2   I tell thee Pandarus;
     When I doe tell thee, there my hopes lye drown'd :
     Reply not in how many Fadomes deepe
     They lye indrench'd.

3   I tell thee, I am mad
     In Cressids love.

4   Thou answer'st she is Faire,
     Powr'st in the open Ulcer of my heart,
     Her Eyes, her Haire, her Cheeke, her [Gate], her Voice,
     Handlest in thy discourse.

5   O that her Hand
     (In whose comparison, all whites are Inke)
     Writing their owne reproach ;   to whose soft seizure,
     The Cignets Downe is harsh, and spirit of Sense
     Hard as the palme of Plough-man.

6   This thou tel'st me ;
     As true thou tel'st me, when I say I love her :
     But saying thus, instead of Oyle and Balme,
     Thou lai'st in every gash that love hath given me,
     The Knife that made it.

• from the very start, in telling Pandarus 'my hopes lye drown'd', Troylus seems agitated, with the two word passionate F #1 (1/1) ending with a rare (for an original Shakespeare printing) exclamation mark, and the emotional F #2 (2/5) being composed entirely of three surround phrases, the first two heightened even further by being linked by an (emotional) semicolon

• however, in explaining the root of the problem, 'I am mad in Cressids love' and how Pandarus is not helping by continuing to talk about her, Troylus seems to regain intellectual control (8/4, F #3-4) – but F's peculiar punctuation suggests that this may only mask how deeply he is still disturbed: most modern texts attempt to clarify the text by setting major punctuation after 'voice' and removing F's period (and Q's colon) after 'discourse' as shown, although this rational re-write doesn't really match Troylus' passion as originally expressed - especially when considering the broken nature of the rest of his comments

• after the broken end to F #4's, as Troylus' focuses on Cressida's hand, he starts passionately (via the first two lines of the new F only #5, 2/2) but the struggle to stay on even keel seems difficult for him to manage, for he seesaws back to intellect (4/2, F #5's last two lines) with the moment of transition marked by the second emotional semicolon of the speech

• certainly the final sentence continues to show this struggle for the calm start

" This thou tel'st me ; /As true thou tel'st me, when I say I love her : "

(its unembellishment doubly weighted by being monosyllabic and made up of two surround phrases), is quickly replaced by a passionate cluster (3/2) as he clarifies just what pain Pandarus has caused him, though interestingly the lead in 'Thou lai'st in every gash that love hath given me' is once more unembellished, as if Troylus can hardly give it voice

The Tragedie of Troylus and Cressida
Achilles

What meane these fellowes? know they not Achilles?

3.3.70 - 94

Background: the Greek commander Ajax has been fooled into join-
ing the anti-Achilles faction (he seriously, they more lightheartedly
but with a very serious purpose underneath): now the commanders,
with Ajax, deliberately walk by Achilles' tent barely giving Achilles
the time of day, leaving Ulysses to follow a little later once Achilles
realises something is wrong, as he now does: Achilles offers the following to his close companion Patroclus

Style: as part of a two-handed scene

Where: outside Achilles' tent

To Whom: Patroclus

# of Lines: 24

Probable Timing: 1.15 minutes

Take Note: In a very emotional speech (5/22), the fact Achilles is
working very hard to understand why he is suddenly out of favour
is underscored by the first fourteen lines being composed almost
entirely of eleven surround phrases and one short sentence, and
the fifteen syllable line ending F #2 suggesting an explosion (which
most modern texts reduce by setting up a much more controlled response (10/5 as shown), establishing a pause where none originally
existed).

Achilles

1   What mean these fellows?

2   Know they not Achilles ?

3   {†}They pass by strangely .

4   They were us'd to bend,
     To send their smiles before them {,}
     To come as humbly as they [use] to creep
     To holy Altars .

5   What, am I poor of late ?

6   'Tis certain, greatness, once fall'n out with fortune,
     Must fall out with men too .

7   What the declin'd is,
     He shall as soon read in the eyes of others,
     As feel in his own fall ; for men, like butterflies,
     Show not their mealy wings but to the summer,
     And not a man, for being simply man,
     Hath any honor, but [honor] for those honors
     That are without him, as place, riches, and favor
     Prizes of accident, as oft as merit,
     Which when they fall, as being slippery standers,
     The love that lean'd on them as slippery too,
     [Do th'one] pluck down another, and together
     Die in the fall .

8   But 'tis not so with me,
     Fortune and I are friends .

9   I do enjoy
     At ample point, all that I did possess,
     Save these men's looks, who do me thinks find out
     Something not worth in me such rich beholding
     As they have often given .

10   Here is Ulysses,
     I'll interrupt his reading .

11   How now, Ulysses ?

Achilles

1 What meane these fellowes ? know they not Achilles ?
2 {†}They passe by strangely : they were us'd to bend
   To send their smiles before them {} :
   To come as humbly as they [us'd] to creepe to holy Altars.
3 What am I poore of late ?
4 'Tis certaine, greatnesse once falne out with fortune,
   Must fall out with men too : what the declin'd is,
   He shall as soone reade in the eyes of others,
   As feele in his owne fall : for men like butter-flies,
   Shew not their mealie wings, but to the Summer :
   And not a man for being simply man,
   Hath any honour ; but honour'd for those honours
   That are without him ; as place, riches, and favour,
   Prizes of accident, as oft as merit :
   Which when they fall, as being slippery standers ;
   The love that leand on them as slippery too,
   [Doth one] plucke downe another, and together
   Dye in the fall.
5   But 'tis not so with me ;
   Fortune and I are friends, I doe enjoy
   At ample point, all that I did possesse,
   Save these mens lookes : who do me thinkes finde out
   Something not worth in me such rich beholding,
   As they have often given.
6   Here is Ulisses,
   lle interrupt his reading : how now Ulisses ?

• the first self-doubts come from the realisation that Agamemnon, Nestor and Ajax who have just passed him by with scant greetings ' ; they were us'd to bend/To send their smiles before them /To come as humbly as . . .' the unembellished quiet adding enormous (startled? horrified?) depth to the realisation, especially when set within the emotional F #1-2, (2/4)

• the only exception to the intense surround phrase start is the two line passage of climactic realisation that results from his previous seven surround phrase self-questioning ' : what the declin'd is,/He shall as soone as reade in the eyes of others,/As feele in his owne fall :', climactic in that this marks an 0/6 three and half line passage opening F #4

• then comes a moment of intellect, the surround phrase pointing to a logical maxim to justify his not venturing himself on any worthless task ": for men like butter-flies,/Shew not their mealie wings, but to the Summer : "

• and then he becomes very quiet (perhaps he is disturbed by these and the ensuing thoughts of quick abandonment) 'Which when they fall, as being slippery standers ; /The love that leand on them as slippery too,' – the unembellished realisation enhanced by being set as yet two more emotional surround phrases – with the final inevitable conclusion of downfall becoming emotional once more (0/3, F #4's last two lines)

• the denial that this could possibly happen to him seems very important and emphatic, being set as an emotional unembellished monosyllabic surround phrase ' . But 'tis not so with me ; ' and the subsequent explanation as to why becomes emotional again (0/4, F #5's last four lines)

• and in an interesting (and determined?) turnaround, Achilles' resolve to do something about the problem (question Ulysses) becomes intellectual (2/0), the decision heightened by being set as two surround phrases - yet the short spelling of Ulysses as 'Ulisses'(twice) suggests Achilles' start may not be quite as confident as he would wish

The Tragedie of Troylus and Cressida
Hector

Thou art great Lord, my Fathers sisters Sonne ;
4.5.120 - 138

Background: through a combination of circumstances Ajax and not
Achilles was chosen for the honour of the single-combat-but-not-
to-the-death challenge with Hector: after the first skirmish Ajax
is more than willing to continue to the fight: however, as Hector
reminds him, as they are related (historically Hector was his uncle)
Hector would rather not continue

Style: one on one address in front of as larger group

Where: the Greek camp

To Whom: Ajax, with, in the background 'all of Troy', including Paris,
Æneas, Helenus and Attendants, and of the Greeks: Agamemnon,
Achilles, Patroclus, Menelaus, Ulysses, Nestor, and 'others'

# of Lines: 19

Probable Timing: 1.00 minutes

Take Note: The opening of this post-fight speech is presented somewhat more rationally by most modern texts, which split the surround phrase riddled onrushed F #1 in two. However, as set, F's
opening, and the overall passion of the speech (19/15 throughout)
could well represent the patterns of someone moderately winded by
the armed combat and genuinely delighted to have crossed swords
honourably with a fine soldier whom has him term a 'cousen'.

Hector

1   Thou art great lord, my father's sister's son,
    A cousin- german to great Priam's seed;
    The obligation of our blood forbids
    A gory emulation 'twixt us twain.

2   Were thy commixtion Greek and [Troyan] so
    That thou couldst say, "This hand is Grecian all,
    And this is [Troyan] ; the sinews of this leg
    All Greek, and this all Troy ; my mother's blood
    Runs on the dexter cheek, and this sinister
    Bounds in my father's" : by Jove multipotent,
    Thou shouldst not bear from me a Greekish member
    Wherein my sword had not impressure made
    Of our rank feud ; but the just gods gainsay
    That any drop thou borrowd'st from thy mother,
    My sacred aunt, should by my mortal sword
    Be drained !

3   Let me embrace thee, Ajax.

4   By him that thunders, thou hast lusty arms !

5   Hector would have them fall upon him thus.

6   Cousin, all honor to thee !

Hector

1　Thou art great Lord, my Fathers sisters Sonne ;
　A cousen german to great Priams seede :
　The obligation of our bloud forbids
　A gorie emulation 'twixt us twaine :
　Were thy commixion, Greeke and [Troian] so,
　That thou could'st say, this hand is Grecian all,
　And this is [Troian] : the sinewes of this Legge,
　All Greeke, and this all Troy : my Mothers bloud
　Runs on the dexter cheeke, and this sinister
　Bounds in my fathers : by Jove multipotent,
　Thou should'st not beare from me a Greekish member
　Wherein my sword had not impressure made
　Of our ranke feud : but the just gods gainsay,
　That any drop thou borrowd'st from thy mother,
　My sacred Aunt, should by my mortall Sword
　Be drained.

2　　　　　　　Let me embrace thee Ajax :
　By him that thunders, thou hast lustie Armes ;
　Hector would have them fall upon him thus.

3　Cozen, all honor to thee.

- the opening public-acknowledgement surround phrases attest to his pleasure

> " . Thou art great Lord, my Fathers sisters Sonne ; /A cousen german to great Priams seede : "

and the mixture of styles, the first intellectual (3/1) the second emotional (1/2) serve to illustrate the conflicting tugs within him, hardly surprising since he is giving due praise to an enemy who is also a relative

- thus the next two line suggestion that since they come from common blood no blood should be spilled is emotional (0/2)

- in eventually (and fancifully, as a joke perhaps?) suggesting that if different body parts of Ajax could be identified as either Greek or Trojan Hector would not allow him to leave with any Greek members intact, Hector at least begins intellectually (4/1, F #1's lines four to half way through line six)

- however, the surround phrase ' : the sinewes of this Legge,/All Greeke, and this all Troy : ' turns the notion up a notch, for the next six lines become passionate (6/6)

- and then, for whatever reason (courtesy? or that the non too bright Ajax takes him seriously?) the unembellished section 'but the just gods gainsay, /That any drop thou borrow'st from thy mother,' leads to a gentle sentence ending avowal that he will not spill Ajax's blood (2/1 F #1's last three lines)

- and in offering to embrace Ajax, the totally surround phrase passionate F #2 (2/2) and short F #3 (1/) reinforce all that Hector has said to date

The Tragedie of Othello, the Moore of Venice
Rodorigo

I do not finde / That thou deal'st justly with me .
between 4.2.173 - 203

Background: Iago's careful plans are not working out to his complete satisfaction: while Othello is in disgrace and the marriage effectively over, Desdemona will never be his and the hated Cassio has been promoted: and now Rodorigo has finally woken up to what Iago has been doing with the money he has given him for gifts to Desdemona, and is about to demand full reparation

Style: as part of a two-handed scene

Where: unspecified, but probably somewhere in the garrison

To Whom: Iago

# of Lines: 20

Probable Timing: 1.00 minutes

Take Note: That there are relatively few releases (7/13 in nineteen lines) in what are very emotional circumstances suggests the character is trying to control himself – a new stage of development for a man whose second scene was one of self-pitying half-hearted threat of committing suicide. However, the fact that he reverts to prose after just two awkward short lines of verse that open the speech suggests the self-control may be causing him considerable strain.

Rodorigo

1　I do not find that thou deal'st justly with me .

2　Every day thou daff'st me with some device,
Iago, and rather, as it seems to [me, thou] keep'st from
me all convenience then suppliest me with the least
ad vantage of hope.

3　　　　　　　　　　I will indeed no longer endure it ;nor
am I yet persuaded to put up in peace what already I
have foolishly suff'red.

4　{†}　　　　　　　　　　Your words and
[performance] are no kin together.

5　　　　　　　　　　　I have wasted myself
out of [ ] means.
　　　　　　　　　The jewels you have had from
me to deliver Desdemona would half have corrupted
a votarist.

6　　　　　You have told me she hath receiv'd them,
and return'd me expectations and comforts of sudden
respect, and [acquittance], but I find none.

7　[By this hand, I say 'tis very] scurvy, and begin to
find myself fopp'd in it.

8　{†}　　　　　　　　　I will make myself
known to Desdemona.

9　　　　　　　　　If she will return me my
jewels, I will give over my suit and repent my unlaw-
ful solicitation ; if not, assure yourself I will seek
satisfaction of you.

10　I {have}said nothing but what I protest intendment of doing.

Rodorigo

1   I do not finde
That thou deal'st justly with me.

---

2   Every day thou dafts me with some devise
Iago, and rather, as it seemes to [me now], keep'st from
me all convenience, then suppliest me with the least
advantage of hope : I will indeed no longer endure it.

3   Nor
am I yet perswaded to put up in peace, what already I
have foolishly suffred.

---

4   {†}   Your words and
[Performances] are no kin together.

---

5   I have wasted my selfe
out of [my] meanes.

6   The Jewels you have had from
me to deliver Desdemona, would halfe have corrupted
a Votarist.

7   You have told me she hath receiv'd them,
and return'd me expectations and comforts of sodaine
respect, and [acquaintance], but I finde none.

---

8   [Nay] I think it is] scurvy : and begin to
finde my selfe fopt in it.

---

9   {†}   I will make my selfe
knowne to Desdemona.

10   If she will returne me my
Jewels, I will give over my Suit, and repent my unlawfull solicitation.

11   If not, assure your selfe, I will seeke
satisfaction of you.

- the few surround phrases point to a character who is standing up for himself for the first time in the play

   " : I will indeed no longer endure it . "

   " . [Nay] I think it is] scurvy : and begin to finde my selfe fopt in it . "

- that his anger/disgust is explained in more detail via the unembellished

   "Your words and Performances are no kin together ."

   " I have said nothing but what I protest intendment of doing."

   is a great indication of how determined he has now become, especially when the unembellished quality of most of the first two surround phrases listed above are added into the equation

- given what Rodorigo has to say, that he manages so much self-control with virtually no releases for the first nine lines of the speech (F #1-4, 1/3) is a great tribute to his determination that, for the first time in the play, he will be the one to take charge of a conversation with Iago

- as long as he focuses on Iago's wrongdoings Rodorigo manages to stay in control, but as soon as he turns to his own concerns releases start coming thick and fast, with F #5's wasting 'my meanes' being emotional (0/2); F #6's that the 'Jewels' given to Iago should have 'corrupted' Desdemona is strongly factual (3/1, in just two lines); while the rebuke that despite Iago's assurances to the contrary he is getting no positive response from Desdemona and thinks Iago is fooling turns him emotional again (F #7-8, 0/3)

- then comes his only passionate moment in the speech, as he states he will confront Desdemona and if she will return his jewels he will apologise for and cease his 'unlawfull solicitation' (F #9-10, 3/3)

- and his facing down of Iago concludes first with an emotional threat that if he doesn't get his jewels back 'I will seeke satisfaction of you' (F #11, 0/2) and F #12's final icy quiet, unembellished, assurance he will do exactly as he has promised

The Tragedie of Macbeth
Malcom/Malcome

What I beleeve, Ile waile ;/What know, beleeve ;
between 4.3.8 - 31

Background: Macduff did indeed flee to England, not to save him-self but in an attempt to bring Malcome, Duncan's oldest son (who was legitimately named king by his father before Macbeth began his murderous attacks) back to Scotland as the leader of a growing number of anti-Macbeth dissidents. However, Malcome has been tempted too often by agents of Macbeth to believe in Macduff's integrity without a great deal of questioning and challenges.

Style: as part of a two-handed scene

Where: somewhere in the English court

To Whom: Macduff

# of Lines: 22

Probable Timing: 1.10 minutes

Take Note: Malcome starts out extraordinarily strongly (even vehe-mently), the emotional opening of his mistrust (0/5, F #1) made even stronger by being set as four consecutive surround phrases,

" . What I beleeve, Ile waile ; /What know, beleeve ; and what I can redresse,/As I shall finde the time to friend : I wil . "

 - the first three even further enhanced by the extra emotional power of the first two semicolons.

Malcom

1   What I believe, I'll wail,
    What know, believe; and what I can redress,
    As I shall find the time to friend, I will.

2   What you have spoke, it may be so perchance .

3   This tyrant, whose sole name blisters our tongues,
    Was once thought honest; you have lov'd him well;
    He hath not touch'd you yet.

4   I am young, but something
    You may [deserve] of him through me, and wisdom
    To offer up a weak, poor, innocent lamb
    T'appease an angry god.

---

5   A good and virtuous nature may recoil
    In an imperial charge.

6   But I shall crave your pardon;
    That which you are, my thoughts cannot transpose:
    Angels are bright still, though the brightest fell.

7   Though all things foul would wear the brows of grace,
    Yet grace must still look so.

---

8   Why in that rawness left you wife, and child,
    Those precious motives, those strong knots of love,
    Without leave-taking ?

9   I pray you,
    Let not my jealousies be your dishonors,
    But mine own safeties.

10   You may be rightly just,
    What ever I shall think.

Malcome

1   What I beleeve, Ile waile ;
    What know, beleeve; and what I can redresse,
    As I shall finde the time to friend: I wil.

2   What you have spoke, it may be so perchance .

3   This Tyrant, whose sole name blisters our tongues,
    Was once thought honest: you have lov'd him well,
    He hath not touch'd you yet.

4   I am yong, but something
    You may [discerne] of him through me, and wisedome
    To offer up a weake, poore innocent Lambe
    T'appease an angry God.

---

5   A good and vertuous Nature may recoyle
    In an Imperiall charge.

6   But I shall crave your pardon :
    That which you are, my thoughts cannot transpose;
    Angels are bright still, though the brightest fell.

7   Though all things foule, would wear the brows of grace
    Yet Grace must still looke so.

---

8   Why in that rawnesse left you Wife, and Childe ?
    Those precious Motives, those strong knots of Love,
    Without leave-taking.

9   I pray you,
    Let not my Jealousies, be your Dishonors,
    But mine owne Safeties: you may be rightly just,
    What ever I shall thinke.

• the drive continues with the short F #2 - suggesting Macduffe might be honest - with F #3's two more surround phrases challenging this assumption because when Macbeth was thought honest Macduffe loved him: in doing so, Malcome becomes very quiet since, save for the word 'Tyrant' (itself a wonderful indicator of his feelings about Macbeth) F #2-3 are unembellished - though whether Malcome is trying to control himself or is just freezing out Macduffe is up to each actor to explore

• F #4's extension that Macduffe may be thus tempted to deliver Malcome to Macbeth is emotional (2/4), in turn triggering passion (2/2) for his damning F #5 suggestion that anyone could prove treacherous 'In an Imperiall charge'

• that Malcome is torn can be seen in the ensuing three surround phrase F #6

> " . But I shall crave your pardon : /That which you are, my
> thoughts cannot transpose ; /Angels are bright still, though
> the brightest fell . "

for not only does the apology/attack seem to be very carefully worded and voiced, in that the sentence is unembellished, it also seems to cause him strain, for the last two surround phrases are again linked by an emotional semicolon

• which leads to yet another emotional elaboration, F #7 suggesting in no uncertain terms that appearances (and therefore Macduffe) can be deceptive (1/2)

• Malcome then becomes slightly more intellectual for the rest of the speech both for the all-important question of why Macduffe so suddenly abandoned his family (F #8, 4/2) and for the F #9 apology for his doubts (3/2)

• after all the doubts, the possibility that Macduffe may be honest is heightened with the last words of the speech, the surround phrase

> " : you may be rightly just,/What ever I shall thinke . "

Macduff

All my pretty ones?/Did you say All?
between 4.3.216 - 234

Background: This is Macduff's immediate response to Rosse's appalling news that Madcuff's family has been murdered.

Style: one on one address with a third person present

Where: somewhere in the English court

To Whom: Rosse, in front of Malcome

# of Lines: 18

Probable Timing: 0.55 minutes

Take Note: Quite remarkably under such extraordinarily emotional circumstances, F's orthography suggests that Macduffe is attempting to control himself with a series of reasoned statements (the whole speech being more intellectual than emotional 17/10), with only minute shifts in F's orthography showing where self-control may be too much for him.

Macduff

1   All my pretty ones ?

2   Did you say all ?

3   O hell-kite !

4   All ?

5   What, all my pretty chickens, and their dam,
    At one fell swoop?

---

6   I shall {dispute it like a man} ;
    But I must also feel it as a man :
    I cannot but remember such things were
    That were most precious to me.

7   Did heaven look on,
    And would not take their part ?

8   Sinful Macduff,
    They were all strook for thee! naught that I am,
    Not for their own demerits, but for mine,
    Fell slaughter on their souls.

9   Heaven rest them now .

---

10 O, I could play the woman with mine eyes,
    And braggart with my tongue !

11   But, gentle heavens,
    Cut short all intermission .

12   Front to front,
    Bring thou this fiend of Scotland and myself;
    Within my sword's length set him ; if he scape
    Heaven forgive him too.

Macduff

1   All my pretty ones ?

2   Did you say All ?

3   Oh Hell-Kite !

4   All ?

5   What, All my pretty Chickens, and their Damme
     At one fell swoope ?

---

6   I shall {dispute it like a man} :
     But I must also feele it as a man;
     I cannot but remember such things were
     That were most precious to me: Did heaven looke on,
     And would not take their part?

7   Sinfull Macduff,
     They were all strooke for thee: Naught that I am,
     Not for their owne demerits, but for mine
     Fell slaughter on their soules:Heaven rest them now.

---

8   O I could play the woman with mine eyes,
     And Braggart with my tongue.

9   But gentle Heavens,
     Cut short all intermission: Front to Front,
     Bring thou this Fiend of Scotland, and my selfe
     Within my Swords length set him, if he scape
     Heaven forgive him too.

- the speech opens with a series of very short sentences (F #1-4) - further proof of his attempt to maintain self-control – each offering the very minimum that need be said, t part of an intellectual start (6/3, F #1-5)

- after the unembellished bulk of F #6 (0/1, the first three and a half lines), the realisation that they were killed for him is the only emotional passage in the speech (3/5, F #6's last line, all of F #7 save the last phrase)

- with the resolve to action that dominates the rest of the speech it seems that Macduffe regains self-control and is very strongly intellectual (8/1. the last six lines of the speech - from the last phrase of F #7 on)

- however, that Macduffe's inner turmoil almost bursts through can be seen in that unlike most modern texts, F ungrammatically, sets no punctuation between F #9's lines three and four ('my selfe' and 'Within my Swords length') suggesting that (the fervency of?) Macduffe's avowal is getting the better of him: for clarity most modern texts add a comma, making the moment far more logical than originally set

- the unembellished passages show where he is working at his hardest to control himself no matter what the internal personal cost - from the very opening " . All my pretty ones ? "

  through to his refusal to give into tears, no matter what, with just the one incredibly telling word 'feele' breaking F #6's three and a half otherwise unembellished lines " . I shall {dispute it like a man} : /But I must also feele it as a man ; /I cannot but remember such things were/That were most precious to me : "

  his calm determination not to give in to his own emotions intensified by the text being set as three (of four) consecutive surround phrases and the momentary breaking of his self control via the impassioned phrase ' : Did heaven looke on', before F #6's last phrase 'And would not take their part' re-establishes self-control once more

- the remaining three surround phrases all point to key realisations or requests : . Sinfull Macduff,/They were all strooke for thee : " " : Heaven rest them now . " " . But gentle Heavens/Cut short all intermission

The Tragedie of King Lear

Bastard

This is the excellent foppery of the world,
1.2.118 - 137

Background: this is Edmund's response to Gloucester's explanation for the strangeness of current events

Style: solo

Where: unspecified, but probably Gloucester's home

To Whom: direct audience address, and self

# of Lines: 19

Probable Timing: 1.00 minutes

Take Note: Having dedicated his services to the goddess Nature it's hardly surprising Edmund has little time for the conventional wisdom of predestined planetary influences and their effects on the world of men – though what may be surprising is how lengthy and full of release his rejection of the doctrine turns out to be.

Bastard

1   This is the excellent foppery of the world, that when
     we are sick in fortune - often the surfeits of our own
     behavior - we make guilty of our disasters the sun, the
     moon, and stars, as if we were villains on necessity,
     fools by heavenly compulsion, knaves, thieves, and
     treachers by spherical predominance;   drunkards, li-
     ars, and adulterers by an enforc'd obedience of planetary
     influence;   and all that we are evil in, by a divine thru-
     sting on.

2   An admirable evasion of whoremaster man,
     to lay his goatish disposition on the charge of a star !

3   My father compounded with my mother under the Dra-
     gon's tail, and my nativity was under Ursa Major, so
     that it follows, I am rough and lecherous.

4   [Fut] I should
     have been that I am, had the maidenl'est star in the fir-
     mament twinkled on my bastardizing.

     Enter Edgar

5   Pat ! he comes like the catastrophe of the old comedy .

6   My cue is villainous melancholy, with a sigh like Tom
     o'Bedlam.

7   _____ O these eclipses do portend these divi-
     sions ! *fa, sol, la, mi.*

Bastard

1   This is the excellent foppery of the world, that when
     we are sicke in fortune, often the surfets of our own
     behaviour, we make guilty of our disasters, the Sun, the
     Moone, and Starres, as if we were villaines on necessitie,
     Fooles by heavenly compulsion, Knaves, Theeves, and
     Treachers by Sphericall predominance.

2   Drunkards, Ly-
     ars, and Adulterers by an inforc'd obedience of Planatary
     influence; and all that we are evill in, by a divine thru-
     sting on.

3   An admirable evasion of Whore-master-man,
     to lay his Goatish disposition on the charge of a Starre,
     My father compounded with my mother under the Dra-
     gons taile, and my Nativity was under Ursa Major, so
     that it followes, I am rough and Leacherous.

4   [ ] I should
     have bin that I am, had the maidenlest Starre in the Fir-
     mament twinkled on my bastardizing.

                    Enter Edgar

5   Pat : he comes like the Catastrophe of the old Comedie :
     my Cue is villanous Melancholly, with a sighe like Tom
     o'Bedlam.

6   _____ O these Eclipses do portend these divi-
     sions.

7   Fa, Sol, La, Me .

• Edmund's dismissal of his father and the world he represents seen in the calm unembellished opening of the speech,

> "This is the excellent foppery of the world,"

might be dismissed as contemptuously easy, except that this, the only unembellished line, triggers a lengthy list of ridiculousness, suggesting he has no time for the belief as the one emotional surround phrase puts it

> " ; and all that we are evill in, by a divine thrusting on . "

• that this has probably been a sore point can be seen in the ungrammatical ending of F #1 - as if something in the next set of descriptions coming up ('Lyar' perhaps?) generates in Edmund a need to pause (anger? amusement? despair?) - most modern texts set a comma, allowing the flow to continue into a larger whole much more smoothly

• thus after the unembellished opening, Edmund starts emotionally (0/2 F #1's first three lines) and then quickly moves into passion as he lists the supposed astrological influences on the world of men (8/6, F #1's last three lines), and while F #2's ungrammatical dismissal of evil coming from 'an inforc'd obedience of Planetary influence' starts intellectually, but the surround phrase already discussed is doubly emotional (0/1)

• Edmund's F #3's five lines (of mockery? amusement? irony?) as he begins to apply this 'Planetary influence' to his own compounding and 'Nativity' is highly intellectual (9/4), but the resultant F #4 terse self-definition becomes passionate (1/1)

• the arrival of his brother (F #5) and the beginning (10/2) of the plan to ensnare him (F #6-7) is strongly intellectual – the assessment of his own inevitable success heightened by the two surround phrases that open F #5

> " . Pat : he comes like the catastrophe of the old Comedie : "

The Tragedie of King Lear
Edgar

I heard my selfe proclaim'd,
2.3.1 - 21

Background: thanks to Edmund's plottings and further trickery, Gloucester has given orders that his legitimate son Edgar should be taken prisoner: the following is spoken as Edgar tries to escape

Style: solo

Where: somewhere in the open

To Whom: direct audience address, and self

# of Lines: 20

Probable Timing: 1.00 minutes

Take Note: Despite the onrushed F #3 which initially suggests Edgar cannot maintain self control, F's orthography shows far more human dignity than modern rationality does (most modern texts having divided F #3 into five); however, Edgar manages to preserve a strong sense of self-identity despite the difficulties facing him.

Edgar

1   I heard myself proclaim'd,
     And by the happy hollow of a tree
     Escap'd the hunt.

2   No port is free, no place
     That guard and most unusual vigilance
     Does not attend my taking.

3   Whiles I may scape
     I will preserve myself, and am bethought
     To take the basest and most poorest shape
     That ever penury, in contempt of man,
     Brought near to beast.

4   My face I'll grime with filth,
     Blanket my loins, elf all my hairs in knots,
     And with presented nakedness outface
     The winds and persecutions of the sky.

5   The country gives me proof and president
     Of Bedlam beggars, who, with roaring voices,
     Strike in their numb'd and mortified arms
     Pins, wooden-pricks, nails, sprigs of rosemary;
     And with this horrible object, from low farms,
     Poor pelting villages, [sheep-cotes], and mills,
     [Sometime] with lunatic bans, sometime with prayers,
     Enforce their charity.

6   Poor Turlygod ! poor Tom !

7   That's something yet : Edgar I nothing am .

Edgar

1   I heard my selfe proclaim'd,
    And by the happy hollow of a Tree,
    Escap'd the hunt.

2   No Port is free, no place
    That guard, and most unusall vigilance
    Do's not attend my taking.

3   Whiles I may scape
    I will preserve myselfe: and am bethought
    To take the basest, and most poorest shape
    That ever penury in contempt of man,
    Brought neere to beast;   my face Ile grime with filth,
    Blanket my loines, elfe all my haires in knots,
    And with presented nakednesse out-face
    The Windes, and persecutions of the skie;
    The Country gives me proofe, and president
    Of Bedlam beggers, who with roaring voices,
    Strike in their num'd and mortified Armes,
    Pins, Wodden-prickes, Nayles, Sprigs of Rosemarie:
    And with this horrible object, from low Farmes,
    Poore pelting Villages, [Sheeps-Coates], and Milles,
    [Sometimes] with Lunaticke bans, sometime with Praiers
    Inforce their charitie: poore Turlygod, poore Tom,
    That's something yet: Edgar I nothing am.

- given the circumstances of the hunt all around him, the few releases in the first four and half lines (2/2, F #1-2) could well suggest Edgar is trying to be as quiet as possible to avoid detection

- Edgar's determination to save himself can be seen in the onrushed F #3's opening surround phrase

   " Whiles I may scape/I will preserve myselfe : "

   and, by the end of the speech, just how much of a non-person he will have to become to do so is just as strongly recognised

   " : poore Turlygod, poore Tom,/That's something yet : Edgar I
      nothing am . "

- and the need to stay quiet to give himself a chance to 'scape' can be seen in F#3's three and a half (almost) unembellished lines as he begins to give voice to his desperate ploy of demeaning disguise

   " and am bethought/To take the basest, and most poorest shape/
      That ever penury in contempt of man,/Brought neere to beast
      ; my face Ile grime with filth,"

   unembellished save for the key word 'neere' to describe how close to humiliation he is prepared to go by being no better than a beast (an appalling thought for any Elizabethan)

- for a moment emotions swamp him (1/5) as he begins to picture how he must abuse his physical appearance to the point of dirty nigh-near nakedness (the three lines before F #2's next semicolon)

- then comes a two-fold surprise, first that in the midst of his problems he still has the wit/political sense to find a (comforting? practical?) parallel to his condition in the 'Bedlam beggers' that the 'Country' presents him, and that in so doing he manages to contain his passion with evident intellectual control as he lists the 'beggers' appearance and treatment that is shortly to be his (17/11, the last nine lines of the speech)

The Tragedie of King Lear

Edgar

Come on Sir,/Heere's the place : stand still :
between 4.6.11 - 27

Background: despite orders to the contrary, Gloucester has helped
Lear evade the vengeful forces of Cornwall and Regan bent on a
'plot of death' against him: as punishment Cornwall has blinded
Gloucester and cast him loose into the countryside: Edgar, still
disguised as Poore Tom, has come across his newly blinded father:
Gloucester, not recognising his voice, has asked Edgar to escort
him to the cliffs at Dover from which he can throw himself in an
act of suicide: to save him, Edgar is pretending they have arrived at
the cliffs, when in fact they are perfectly safe elsewhere

Style: as part of a two-handed scene

Where: near the cliffs at Dover

To Whom: his blinded father Gloucester

# of Lines: 18

Probable Timing: 0.55 minutes

Edgar

1   Come on, sir, here's the place ; stand still .

2   How fearful
     And dizzy 'tis, to cast one's eyes so low !

3   The crows and choughs that wing the midway air
     Show scarce so gross as beetles.

4   Half way down
     Hangs one that gathers sampire, dreadful trade !
     Methinks he seems no bigger [than] his head .

5   The fishermen, that [walk] upon the beach
     Appear like mice;   and yond tall anchoring bark,
     Diminish'd to her cock;   her cock, a buoy
     Almost too small for sight.

6   The murmuring surge,
     That on th'unnumb'red idle pebble chafes,
     Cannot be heard so high.

7   I'll look no more,
     Least my brain turn, and the deficient sight
     Topple down headlong.

---

8   Give me your hand .

9   You are now within a foot
     Of th'extreme verge.

10   For all beneath the moon
     Would I not leap upright.

Edgar

1   Come on Sir, →
    Heere's the place: stand still: how fearefull
    And dizie 'tis, to cast ones eyes so low,
    The Crowes and Choughes, that wing the midway ayre
    Shew scarse so grosse as Beetles.

2   Halfe way downe
    Hangs one that gathers Sampire: dreadfull Trade:
    Me thinkes he seemes no bigger [then] his head.

3   The Fishermen, that [walk'd] upon the beach
    Appeare like Mice: and yond tall Anchoring Barke,
    Diminish'd to her Cocke: her Cocke, a Buoy
    Almost too small for sight.

4   The murmuring Surge,
    That on th'unnumbred idle Pebble chafes
    Cannot be heard so high.

5   Ile looke no more,
    Least my braine turne, and the deficient sight
    Topple downe headlong.

---

6   Give me your hand :
    You are now within a foote of th'extreme Verge:
    For all beneath the Moone would I not leape upright.

• most modern texts follow Q and form one line from the opening two short lines of Edgar: the F setting (three/eight syllables) allows for careful 'pretend' maneuvering to convince Gloucester they are indeed on a hill, a play-acting heightened by the opening being also set as two surround phrases ". Come on Sir,/Heere's the place : stand still : "

and this opening care might well explain the remaining onrush of the sentence in that having caught his father's attention now, by maintaining an unbroken stream of energy, he can fool Gloucester into accepting the deception (most modern texts break F #1 into three)

• F #2 and #3 are equally determined, setting up the supposed details of what lies way below via six consecutive surround phrases

• however, whereas the passion of the opening onrushed sentence borders on the emotional (4/6, F #1) as if Edgar were fighting hard not to let his emotions cloud his words and actions, by the time of F #2-3's piling on of details the pattern is reversed (7/4) as if he has succeeded

• the sudden intellect of F #4 (2/0) is surprising, but perhaps the newly blinded Gloucester has been trying to use his hearing to verify what Edgar has been talking about, hence the quick unexpected comment they are too high to hear even the surf

• then, in the attempt to distract his father/prevent him from discovering the ruse, Edgar's F #5 'Ile looke no more' becomes purely emotional (0/4), though whether this is play-acting emotion or genuine in the moment for his father to 'leap' is upon them is up to each actor to explore

• just as he opened, Edgar closes with an onrush as he leads Gloucester to the supposed edge: and in addition to the added tension of the onrush (not maintained by most modern texts which often split F #8 in three)

a/ the opening unembellished surround phrase' . Give me your hand : ' conveys great care, and the pause that follows the F only setting of this as a short line allows to maneuver Gloucester into position

b/ the rest of the sentence being set as two surround phrases (2/3) points to the determined focus Edgar displays to the very end

The Tragedie of King Lear

Bastard

To both these Sisters have I sworne my love :
5.1.55 - 69

Background: Edmund's trickery didn't stop with getting rid of brother Edgar: he then betrayed his father Gloucester to the Duke of Cornwall who stripped Gloucester of his title and holdings, gave them to Edmund as reward and then, as the final coup de grace, as punishment blinded Gloucester: but, as the following speech explains, this still isn't enough for Edmund, to whom loyalty means absolutely nothing, for he has wooed both Gonerill and Regan - and they are publicly fighting over him: one note, though Gonerill is still married to the weak Albany, Regan is now a widow (for Cornwall was killed as he blinded Gloucester)

Style: solo

Where: the camp of the English army formed to reject Cordelia's attempt to rescue her father

To Whom: direct audience address

# of Lines: 15

Probable Timing: 0.50 minutes

Take Note: F shows the relaxation, and occasional flurries, of the man who would be alpha-male - though the final moment in contemplating the deaths of Lear and Cordelia suggest he may not be totally immune to feeling.

Bastard

1   To both these sisters have I sworn my love ;
    Each jealous of the other, as the stung
    Are of the adder.

2   Which of them shall I take ?

3   Both ? one ? or neither ?

4   Neither can be enjoy'd
    If both remain alive: to take the widow
    Exasperates, makes mad her sister Goneril,
    And hardly shall I carry out my side,
    Her husband being alive.

5   Now then, we'll use
    His countenance for the battle, which being done,
    Let her who would be rid of him devise
    His speedy taking off.

6   As for the mercy
    Which he intends to Lear and to Cordelia,
    The battle done, and they within our power,
    Shall never see his pardon;   for my state
    Stands on me to defend, not to debate.

Bastard

1 To both these Sisters have I sworne my love :
   Each jealous of the other, as the stung
   Are of the Adder.

2   Which of them shall I take?

3 Both?

4   One?

5   Or neither?

6   Neither can be enjoy'd
   If both remaine alive: To take the Widdow,
   Exasperates, makes mad her Sister Gonerill,
   And hardly shall I carry out my side,
   Her husband being alive.

7   Now then, wee'l use
   His countenance for the Battaile, which being done,
   Let her who would be rid of him, devise
   His speedy taking off.

8   As for the mercie
   Which he intends to Lear and to Cordelia,
   The Battaile done, and they within our power,
   Shall never see his pardon: for my state,
   Stands on me to defend, not to debate.

• the surround phrases and short sentences neatly encapsulate the love triangle " . To both these Sisters have I sworne my love : "

• the (delighted? amazed? mischievous) passion of this opening line (1/1) is followed by the surprisingly calm detachment (0/1) of

> " . Which of them shall I take? /Both? One? Or neither? Neither can be enjoy'd/If both remaine alive : "

suggesting more than careful analysis (relaxed amusement perhaps?)

• however, the danger of making a play for Cornwall's widow Regan is heightened by being voiced with much release (4/2) in just the next line and half

• yet his ability to maintain strong self-control quickly reasserts itself, for calm detachment reappears in his ensuing unembellished admission he cannot make a move on Gonerill, 'And hardly shall I carry out my side,/Her husband being alive.'

• . . . at least until after he has used her husband's forces to his own advantage – and though this suddenly admitted subplot is emotional, (1/2, F #7's first line) he once more establishes calm detachment as he voices his intention to stand aloof so as not be incriminated in anything Gonerill might do to her husband Albany,

> "Let her who would be rid of him, devise/His speedy taking off."

• as he analyses most other of his male rivals throughout the play for their weaknesses and how to combat them (notably his father and brother Edgar), here his dismissal of Albany is intellectual (3/1, F #8's first three lines) – though the reason for getting rid of Lear and Cordelia (his own advancement) is spoken of icily unembellishedly

> " : for my state,/Stands on me to defend, not to debate . "

determination? or perhaps the seriousness in planning the death of a monarch and his daughter, herself the wife of a King, forces him to quiet?

The Tragedy of Coriolanus
Coriolanus

Let them pull all about mine eares, present me
between 3.2.1 - 16

Background: the public anti-Coriolanus sentiment has grown so strong that his supporters know the only way to try to save him is by suggesting they will bring him 'in peace,/Where he shall answer by a lawfull forme/(In peace) to his utmost perill', to the 'Market place': there's just one snag, Coriolanus is not prepared to back down or apologise from the sentiments earlier expressed

Style: group address and one on one in front of the group

Where: Volumnia's home

To Whom: the nobles supporting Coriolanus, and then his mother Volumnia

# of Lines: 15

Probable Timing: 0.50 minutes

Take Note: The entrenchment of Coriolanus' belief that he will never change is underscored by the monosyllabic, emotional (created by the only semicolon), single surround phrase in the speech, vowing no matter what the common people do to him ' ; yet will I still /Be thus to them . ' and the final monosyllabic sentence refusing to be false to his nature, 'Rather say, I play/The man I am.'

Coriolanus

1   Let them pull all about mine ears, present me
     Death on the wheel, or at wild horses' heels,
     Or pile ten hills on the Tarpeian rock,
     That the precipitation might down stretch
     Below the beam of sight, yet will I still
     Be thus to them.

---

2   I muse my mother
     Does not approve me further, who was wont
     To call them woollen vassals, things created
     To buy and sell with groats, to show bare heads
     In congregations to yawn, be still, and wonder,
     When one but of my ordinance stood up
     To speak of peace or war.

3   I talk of you :
     Why did you wish me milder?

4   Would you have me
     False to my nature?

5   Rather say, I play
     The man I am.

Coriolanus

1　Let them pull all about mine eares, present me
　　Death on the Wheele, or at wilde Horses heeles,
　　Or pile ten hilles on the Tarpeian Rocke,
　　That the precipitation might downe stretch
　　Below the beame of sight; yet will I still
　　Be thus to them.

2　　　　　　　　　　I muse my Mother
　　Do's not approve me further, who was wont
　　To call them Wollen Vassailes, things created
　　To buy and sell with Groats, to shew bare heads
　　In Congregations, to yawne, be still, and wonder,
　　When one but of my ordinance stood up
　　To speake of Peace, or Warre.

3　　　　　　　　　　　　　　I talke of you,
　　Why did you wish me milder?

4　　　　　　　　　　　　　Would you have me
　　False to my Nature?

5　　　　　　　　　　　Rather say, I play
　　The man I am.

• thus as he starts to make his I-am-I declaration, it's not surprising the speech opens intellectually (8/4, F #1's opening four and half lines)

• fascinatingly, before his mother's entry, his expression that he is wondering why 'my Mother/Do's not approve me further' in his scornful put-down of the common people when so often she has done the same is fully released, and quite emotionally-passionate (4/7, in the six lines of F #2)

• yet when Volumnia enters he clamps down on both his sentence lengths (now becoming very short) and releases, which he almost completely eradicates

• F #3 is emotional only when he admits in the first phrase 'I talke of you' (0/1), and then he becomes completely quiet in the unembellished asking why she wishes him milder (a far cry from the passion of the previous sentence when she wasn't present)

• his F #4 challenge does she wish him to be false is only slightly more released, this time intellectually (1/0)

• and his final self-definition is quietly defiant, as unembellished as the self definition which ended F #1 before his mother joined them

The Tragedy of Coriolanus

Coriolanus

You common cry of Curs, whose breath I hate,
3.3.118 - 135

Background: all the appeasing advice has gone for naught, for once
in the market place Coriolanus' short temper has got the best of
him again, and he has insulted both the people and the Tribunes,
yet again: Sicinius has therefore pronounced Coriolanus' exile, or
worse ('In the name a'th'people,/And in the power of us the Tribunes, wee/(Ev'n from this instant) banish him our Citie/In
perill of precipitation/From off the Rocke Tarpeian, never more/
To enter our Rome gates./I'th'Peoples name,/I say it shall bee so):
the following is Coriolanus' reply

Style: public address

Where: the Market-place

To Whom: all present, supporters and foes alike

# of Lines: 16

Probable Timing: 0.50 minutes

Take Note: Having been tricked into anger, far from abasing himself,
Coriolanus' initiates an unrelenting passionate attack (13/15 overall), and though seemingly logical, F's orthography reveals two
rather surprising moments at speech's end.

Coriolanus

1   You common cry of curs, whose breath I hate
    As reek a'th'rotten fens, whose loves I prize
    As the dead carcasses of unburied men
    That do corrupt my air - I banish you !
    And here remain with your uncertainty!

2   Let every feeble rumor shake your hearts !
    Your enemies, with nodding of their plumes,
    Fan you into despair !

3   Have the power still
    To banish your defenders, till at length
    Your ignorance (which finds not till it feels,
    Making but reservation of yourselves,
    Still your own foes) deliver you as most
    Abated captives to some nation
    That won you without blows!

4   Despising,
    For you, the city, thus I turn my back;
    There is a world elsewhere .

Coriolanus

1   You common cry of Curs, whose breath I hate,
As reeke a'th'rotten Fennes :   whose Loves I prize,
As the dead Carkasses of unburied men,
That do corrupt my Ayre : I banish you,
And heere remaine with your uncertaintie .

2   Let every feeble Rumor shake your hearts :
Your Enemies, with nodding of their Plumes
Fan you into dispaire : Have the power still
To banish your Defenders, till at length
Your ignorance (which findes not till it feeles,
Making but reservation of your selves,
Still your owne Foes) deliver you
As most abated Captives,   to some Nation
That wonne you without blowes, despising
For you the City .

3   Thus I turne my backe ;
There is a world elsewhere .

• the initial passionate attack (7/7, F #1 and the first two and a half lines of F #2, seven and a half lines in all) is heightened by four surround phrases

" . You common cry of Curs, whose breath I hate, /As reeke a'th'rotten Fennes : . . . : I banish you, And heere remaine with your uncertaintie . /Let every feeble Rumor shake your hearts : /Your Enemies, with nodding of their Plumes/Fan you into dispaire : "

• and even when the drive of the surround phrases stops, the continuation of the onrushed F #2 condemning the Citizens to have all the 'power still/To banish your Defenders' so that these 'Curs' can become 'most abated Captives, to some Nation/That wonne you without blowes' still remains passionate (6/6, F #2's last seven lines)

• and then according to F it seems that Coriolanus finally loses self-control, for whereas most modern texts start their final sentence logically with the phrase 'despising/For you the City', relating it to how Coriolanus feels about them, F, ungrammatically in the opinion of most modern editors, sets the phrase at the end of the may-you-become-captives sequence, thus attaching it to whichever Nation that captures them, thus suggesting the captors will hate Rome because of the common folk that now dominate it

• this triggers an emotional start to his farewell, with F #3 being set as two emotional surround phrases

" . Thus I turne my backe ; /There is a world elsewhere. "

the emotion of the first phrase intensified by the releases (0/2)

• but, in a moment of supreme self-control, his very last words before leaving, 'There is a world elsewhere.', display enormous and perhaps surprising dignity for they are completely unembellished

The Tragedy of Coriolanus
Auffidius

Read it not Noble Lords,/But tell the Traitor
between 5.6.83 - 119

Background: Coriolanus has acceded to his mother's request, and
turned back from Rome and returned to Volscia, knowing this will
probably lead to his death ('Oh my Mother, Mother: Oh!/You have
won a happy victory to Rome./But for your Sonne, beleeve it: Oh
beleeve it,/Most dangerously you have with him prevail'd,/If not
most mortall to him'): and, back in Volscia, as he presents to the
leading Senators an extremely favourable peace proposal for the
Volscians already agreed to by the Romans Coriolanus' prescience
proves correct

Style: a general as well as one on one address

Where: at the Volscian Senate

To Whom: the Volscian Senators and Coriolanus

# of Lines: 20

Probable Timing: 1.00 minutes

Take Note: In a speech where Auffidius no longer has to hold back,
what is remarkable is how carefully he handles the destruction of
Coriolanus, keeping his emotions in check virtually throughout –
the only break in his intellectual control coming at the very end of
the speech.

Auffidius

1   Read it not, noble lords,
     But tell the traitor {Martius}, in the highest degree
     He hath abus'd your powers.

---

2   [Ay] Martius, Caius Martius !

3   Dost thou think
     I'll grace thee with that robbery, thy stol'n name
     Coriolanus, in Corioles?

4   You lords and heads a'th'state, perfidiously
     He has betray'd your business, and given up
     For certain drops of salt, your city Rome,
     I say "your city", to his wife and mother,
     Breaking his oath and resolution like
     A twist of rotten silk, never admitting
     Counsel a'th'war; but at his nurse's tears
     He whin'd and roar'd away your victory,
     That pages blush'd at him, and men of heart
     Look'd wond'ring each at others.

---

5   Why, noble lords,
     Will you be put in mind of his blind fortune,
     Which was your shame, by this unholy braggart,
     'Fore your own eyes and ears?

6 {†} Let him die for't .

Auffidius

1 Read it not Noble Lords,
But tell the Traitor {Martius} in the highest degree
He hath abus'd your Powers.

---

2 [I] Martius, Caius Martius : Do'st thou thinke
Ile grace thee with that Robbery, thy stolne name
Coriolanus in Corioles?

3 You Lords and Heads a'th' State, perfidiously
He ha's betray'd your businesse, and given up
For certaine drops of Salt, your City Rome :
I say your City to his Wife and Mother,
Breaking his Oath and Resolution, like
A twist of rotten Silke, never admitting
Counsaile a'th' warre : But at his Nurses teares
He whin'd and roar'd away your Victory,
That Pages blush'd at him, and men of heart
Look'd wond'ring each at others.

---

4 Why Noble Lords,
Will you be put in minde of his blinde Fortune,
Which was your shame, by this unholy Braggart?
'Fore your owne eyes, and eares?

5 {†} Let him dye for't.

• F #1's opening denial/challenge to Martius is totally intellectual (5/0)

• Auffidius' F #2's onrushed denial even of Martius new-given name at the Volscian expense, 'Coriolanus' is also highly intellectual (7/1)

• as is the lengthy unflattering description to the Volscian Senators of how Martius gave away 'your City Rome' for 'certaine drops of Salt', i.e. 'his Nurses teares' (referring to his mother Volumnia) . . .

• . . . the two F only colons add extra strength to the key descriptions ': I say your City' and ': But at his Nurses teares' , and thus heighten the overall intellect of the F #3 sentence (16/6)

• fascinatingly the one clustered release of (emotional) long spellings seems to point to his own loss of face in being excluded from campaign plans, for the release underscores Coriolanus' 'never admitting/Counsaile a'th'warre : ' (0/2)

• however, having made his report/attack, Auffidius' plea for action (F #4) is passionate (4/4)

• while the final plea for the long hoped for end to all his waiting and watching is the short emotional monosyllabic

> 'Let him dye for't." (F #5, 0/1)

The Tragedie of Anthony and Cleopatra

Cæsar

Why have you stoln upon us thus? you come not
3.6.40 - 55

Background: at Octavia's request she has journeyed back to her brother in Rome as a 'most weake . . . reconciler': the following is Cæsar's immediate reaction to her, in his eyes, under-heralded and inadequately ceremonial appearance

Style: one on one in front of a larger group

Where: Rome, perhaps at Cæsar's palace

To Whom: his sister Octavia, in front of her 'traine' and Agrippa and Mecenas

# of Lines: 14

Probable Timing: 0.45 minutes

Take Note: Given the enormity of the images, the fact that Octavius is more intellectual than emotional virtually throughout (14/7) suggests that for some reason he is holding himself in check (trying not upset his beloved sister perhaps) – yet at times emotion and passion do break through, giving the lie to his self-control.

Cæsar

1   Why have you stol'n upon us thus ?

2   You come not
     Like Cæsar's sister.

3   The wife of Antony
     Should have an army for an usher, and
     The neighs of horse to tell of her approach,
     Long ere she did appear; the trees by th'way
     Should have borne men, and expectation fainted,
     Longing for what it had not ; nay, the dust
     Should have ascended to the roof of heaven,
     Rais'd by your populous troops.

4   But you are come
     A market-maid to Rome, and have prevented
     The ostentation of our love, which, left unshown,
     Is often left unlov'd.

5   We should have met you
     By sea, and land, supplying every stage
     With an augmented greeting

Cæsar

1   Why have you stoln upon us thus ?you come not
    Like Cæsars Sister.

2   The wife of Anthony
    Should have an Army for an Usher, and
    The neighes of Horse to tell of her approach,
    Long ere she did appeare.

3   The trees by th'way
    Should have borne men, and expectation fainted,
    Longing for what it had not .

4   Nay, the dust
    Should have ascended to the Roofe of Heaven,
    Rais'd by your populous Troopes : But you are come
    A Market-maid to Rome, and have prevented
    The ostentation of our love ; which left unshewne,
    Is often left unlov'd : we should have met you
    By Sea, and Land, supplying every Stage
    With an augmented greeting

• the shock of the perceived insult to him, as well as her, in her lack of a flamboyant entourage can be seen in the surround phrases that open the speech, especially the first which is both monosyllabic and unembellished - as if Octavius can barely find his voice - the second finishing with two final words of intellectual flourish (2/0) of (prideful?) self-definition

• his intellect continues in the description of what Octavia should have, 'an Army for an Usher' (3/0, F #2's first line and half), and the suggestion that the 'neighes of Horse' from far away and her route crowded with people even hanging in the trees should mark her arrival turns emotional (1/3, the last two lines of F #2, and F #3)

• and his grandiose notion that the dust of those accompanying her 'Should have ascended to the Roofe of Heaven' turns passionate (3/2, F #4's first two lines)

• but in returning to the perceived insult of Anthony's not allowing her sufficient public display, 'you are come/A Market-maid to Rome', and how he would have received her 'supplying every Stage/With an augmented greeting.' Octavius regains almost full mental discipline (5/1)

• the one slip into emotion (0/1), heightened by being set as an emotional (semicoloned) surround phrase, concerns his belief of how (his) love should be shown as a matter of 'ostentation'

" ; which left unshewne,/Is often left unlov'd : "

and that he so quickly recovers intellectual equilibrium underscores his (desire to be seen as in?) self-control

The Tragedie of Anthony and Cleopatra
Cæsar

He calles me Boy, and chides as he had power
between 4.1.1 – 16 4.6.7 - 9

Background: in a show of old-fashioned chivalry, Anthony has sent a challenge of single hand-to-hand combat to Cæsar: the following expected pragmatic (if not downright cynical) response: this speech is Cæsar's initial assessment of the situation

Style: part of a three-handed scene in front of a larger group

Where: Cæsar's camp, presumably near Alexandria

To Whom: Agrippa and Mecenas, in front of their army

# of Lines: 15

Probable Timing: 0.50 minutes

Take Note: F's orthography shows Octavius' mercurial nature, his switches in style matching his equally swift switches from topic to topic.

Cæsar

1　He calls me boy, and chides as he had power
　　To beat me out of Egypt.

2　　　　　　　　　　　My messenger
　　He hath whipt with rods, dares me to personal combat,
　　Cæsar to Antony .

3　　　　　　　　Let the old ruffian know
　　I have many other ways to die;　mean time
　　Laugh at his challenge.

4　　　　　　　Let our best heads know
　　That to-morrow, the last of many battles
　　We mean to fight.

5　　　　　　　　Within our files there are,
　　Of those that serv'd Mark Antony but late,
　　Enough to fetch him in.

---

one sentence　6　{Go charge Agrippa,

insert from　　　　Plant those that have revolted in the [van],

Act 4 Scene 6　　That Antony may seem to spend his fury
　　　　　　　　Upon himself. }

7　　　　　　　　　　　　See it done,
　　And feast the army ;　we have store to do't,
　　And they have earn'd the waste.

8　　　　　　　　　　　　Poor Antony !

Cæsar

1　He calles me Boy, and chides as he had power
　To beate me out of Egypt .

2　　　　　　　　　　　　　My Messenger
　He hath whipt with Rods, dares me to personal Combat .

3　Cæsar to Anthony : let the old Ruffian know,
　I have many other wayes to dye : meane time
　Laugh at his Challenge .

4　　　　　　　　　　　Let our best heads know,
　That to morrow, the last of many Battailes
　We meane to fight .

5　　　　　　　　　　Within our Files there are,
　Of those that serv'd Marke Anthony but late,
　Enough to fetch him in .

---

one sentence　6　{Go charge Agrippa,

insert from　　　Plant those that have revolted in the [Vant],

Act 4 Scene 6　That Anthony may seeme to spend his Fury
　　　　　　　　Upon himselfe .}

7　　　　　　　　　　　　See it done,
　And Feast the Army, we have store to doo't,
　And they have earn'd the waste .

8　　　　　　　　　　　Poore Anthony .

• Octavius' assessment/response to Anthony's message/challenge opens passionately (F #1, 2/2)

• but his description of what happened to his unfortunate diplomat Thidias is purely intellectual (F #2, 3/0), whether this denotes (amused?) acceptance or his reading of the information for the first time is up to each actor to explore

• normally set as the end to the previous sentence by most modern texts, the ungrammatical start to F #3 ('Cæsar to Anthony'), could well support (amused again?) amazement or disbelief, especially since the information contained in the passionate sentence it opens (3/3, F #3)

　　" . Cæsar to Anthony : let the old Ruffian know,/I have many
　　　　other wayes to dye : meane time/Laugh at his Challenge . "

is heightened by being set as three consecutive surround phrases, the only ones in the speech

• F #4's determination that tomorrow will be 'the last of many Battailes' is slightly emotional (1/2) – while the strategically brilliant if heartless idea of gaining advantage by putting all the men that have deserted Anthony in the front line of the troops that will now oppose him is highly intellectual (7/3, F #5-6) – and whether this is a cold-hearted factual suggestion, or a sudden new idea is up to each actor to explore

• the final instruction to feed the Army before the battle is still slightly intellectual (2/1, F #7)

• and, perhaps surprisingly, so is the final short two word sentence about Anthony, though again whether this is in anticipation of Octavius' expected victory or a final comment on Anthony's message/challenge so easily dismissed earlier is a matter of actor exploration and choice

The Tragedie of Cymbeline

Iachimo

What are men mad ? Hath Nature given them eyes
between 1.6.32 - 50

Background: arriving in Britain, Iachimo wastes no time in attempting to win his bet by seducing Imogen, making his overtures at
their very first meeting: each speech is self-explanatory, the first
general speech of amazement implying Posthumus' foolishness in
choosing another, and the second far more intimate and specific

Style: as part of a two-handed scene

Where: somewhere in the palace

To Whom: Imogen

# of Lines: 18

Probable Timing: 0.55 minutes

Take Note: Iachimo's first (and in terms of imagery, very dense) attempts at softening up Imogen for seduction show great skill, for
not only is the overall speech strongly intellectual (21/9 in just
seventeen lines), four of the six sentences open with great bite: F
#1 is a very short sentence, monosyllabic and unembellished; F #3
and #4 open out with unembellished surround phrases; and F #6's
strong imagery of sexual corruption is composed totally of (three)
surround phrases.

Iachimo

1   What, are men mad ?

2   Hath nature given them eyes
    To see this vaulted arch and the rich crop
    Of sea and land, which can distinguish 'twixt
    The fiery orbs above, and the twinn'd stones
    Upon the number'd beach, and can we not
    Partition make with spectacles so precious
    Twixt fair and foul ?

---

3   It cannot be i'th'eye : for apes and monkeys
    'Twixt two such she's would chatter this way, and
    Contemn with mows the other ; nor i'th'judgment :
    For idiots in this case of favor would
    Be wisely definite : nor i'th'appetite :
    Sluttery, to such neat excellence oppos'd,
    Should make desire vomit emptiness,
    Not so allur'd to feed .

---

4   The cloyed will,
    That satiate yet unsatisfied desire, that tub
    Both fill'd and running - ravening first the lamb,
    Longs after for the garbage .

Iachimo

1   What are men mad ?

2   Hath Nature given them eyes
   To see this vaulted Arch, and the rich Crop
   Of Sea and Land, which can distinguish 'twixt
   The firie Orbes above, and the twinn'd Stones
   Upon the number'd Beach, and can we not
   Partition make with Spectacles so pretious
   Twixt faire, and foule ?

---

3   It cannot be i'th'eye : for Apes, and Monkeys
   'Twixt two such She's, would chatter this way, and
   Contemne with mowes the other .

4   Nor i'th'judgment :
   For Idiots in this case of favour, would
   Be wisely definit : Nor i'th'Appetite .

5   Sluttery to such neate Excellence, oppos'd
   Should make desire vomit emptinesse,
   Not so allur'd to feed .

---

6   The Cloyed will :
   That satiate yet unsatisfi'd desire, that Tub
   Both fill'd and running : Ravening first the Lambe,
   Longs after for the Garbage .

• the fact the most modern texts create a single mt. #3 offers an on-rushed blurt instead of allowing each of F #3, #4 and #5 to stand independently: thus most modern Iachimos already seem to be on a roll whereas their original counter-parts seem to be working far harder-in an attempt to get their overly-dense imagery understood

• and the five extra breath-thoughts scattered through the piece add extra support to the original Iachimo's extra hard work

• the only crack in the intellectual barrage is F #5's (1/2) as he begins to become somewhat more specific, comparing Posthumus' supposed object of dalliance ('Sluttery') to the purity of Imogen (described as 'Excellence')

The Tragedie of Cymbeline

Iachimo

Had I this cheeke/To bathe my lips upon : this hand, whose touch,
between 1.6.99 - 117

Background: arriving in Britain, Iachimo wastes no time in attempting to win his bet by seducing Imogen, making his overtures at their very first meeting: each speech is self-explanatory, the first general speech of amazement implying Posthumus' foolishness in choosing another, and the second far more intimate and specific

Style: as part of a two-handed scene

Where: somewhere in the palace

To Whom: Imogen

6 # of Lines: 18

Probable Timing: 0.55 minutes

Take Note: That the intellect of the first seduction attempt (prior speech, 21/9) may not have gone down as well as expected is shown by the totally different set of releases in this second speech (5/15 in the first two sentences, 5/5 in the last).

Iachimo

1   Had I this cheek
To bath my lips upon ; this hand, whose touch
(Whose every touch) which force the feeler's soul
To th'oath of loyalty ; this object, which
Takes prisoner the wild motion of mine eye,
[Fixing] it only here; should I (damn'd then)
Slaver with lips as common as the stairs
That mount the Capitol; join grips with hands
Made hard with hourly falsehood (falsehood , as
With labor) ; then by-peeping in an eye
Base and illustrious as the smoky light
That's fed with stinking tallow : it were fit
That all the plagues of hell should at one time
Encounter such revolt .

---

2   {t}   {Your} Lord, I fear,
Has forgot Britain .

3   And himself.

4   Not I
Inclin'd to this intelligence, pronounce
The beggary of his change ; but 'tis your graces
That from my mutest conscience to my tongue
Charms this report out .

Iachimo

1   Had I this cheeke
     To bathe my lips upon : this hand, whose touch,
     (Whose every touch) which force the Feelers soule
     To'th'oath of loyalty .

2   This object, which
     Takes prisoner the wild motion of mine eye,
     [Fiering] it onely heere, should I (damn'd then)
     Slavver with lippes as common as the stayres
     That mount the Capitoll : Joyne gripes, with hands
     Made hard with hourely falshood (falshood as
     With labour :) then by peeping in an eye
     Base and illustrious as the smoakie light
     That's fed with stinking Tallow : it were fit
     That all the plagues of Hell should at one time
     Encounter such revolt .

---

3   {†}   {Your} Lord, I feare
     Has forgot Brittaine .

4   And himselfe, not I
     Inclin'd to this intelligence, pronounce
     The Beggery of his change : but 'tis your Graces
     That from my mutest Conscience, to my tongue,
     Charmes this report out .

- the differences are especially apparent as the speech opens, for as Iachimo starts to zero in on Imogen herself (her 'cheeke' and 'hand'), F #1 's surround phrase start is far more emotional than anything in the previous speech (1/3) - and this is just the prelude to the middle of F #2

- having moved his focus from her cheek to her hand and wishing to expand further, he needs a new sentence (ungrammatical as far as most modern texts are concerned), the move at first causing him to go enormously quiet (F #2's first line and half opening without embellishment)

- unlike the first speech, here the imagery has been clear, at least until now – but then he returns to incredible complexity as he hints at Posthumus' supposed brushes with prostitutes, bursting into a huge emotional release (2/11, F #2's next four and half lines) as he laments how her hand has been/might be cheapened

- though he manages to calm down somewhat by sentence end (perhaps for effect, pretending he has been moved at the thought of Posthumus' foolishness - 2/1, F #2's last four and a half lines) – the complex imagery still remains

- however, in stating directly that Posthumus has forgotten Britain (and, by implication) thus Imogen herself, Iachimo manages to regain his initial simplicity

- and as he does so, passion returns (5/4, F #3-4), the final extra breath-thoughts in the penultimate line suggesting (whether truthfully or for effect) his (supposed?) awkwardness/embarrassment in having to be the bearer of such disquieting news

The Tragedie of Cymbeline

Cloten

If she be up, Ile speake with her : if not
2.3.64 - 76

Background: encouraged by his mother and step-father King
Cymbeline, Cloten still insists on wooing Imogen, even though
she's married and cannot stand him: the following occurs after his
early morning serenade outside Imogen's window (musicians and
all), has failed to yield any response

Style: solo

Where: outside Imogen's bedroom window or door

To Whom: direct audience address

# of Lines: 13

Probable Timing: 0.45 minutes

Take Note: For an early morning speech, the onrushed nature of F
#1 (split into five sentences by most modern texts) and three sur-
round phrases opening F #1 plus two closing it, point to just how
much unchecked release accompanies anything that Cloten tries
to achieve . . .

Cloten

1   If she be up, I'll speak with her ; if not,
    Let her lie still and dream .

2   By your leave ho !

3   I know her women are about her ; what
    If I do line one of their hands ?

4   'Tis gold
    Which buys admittance (oft it doth), yea, and makes
    Diana's rangers false themselves, yield up
    Their deer to th'stand o'th'stealer ; and 'tis gold
    Which makes the true man kill'd and saves the thief;
    Nay, sometime hangs both thief and true man .

5   What
    Can it not do, and undo ?

6   I will make
    One of her women lawyer to me, for
    I yet not understand the case myself .

7   By your leave .

Cloten

1   If she be up, Ile speake with her : if not
     Let her lye still, and dreame : by your leave hoa,
     I know her women are about her : what
     If I do line one of their hands, 'tis Gold
     Which buyes admittance (oft it doth) yea, and makes
      Diana's Rangers false themselves, yeeld up
     Their Deere to'th'stand o'th'Stealer : and 'tis Gold
     Which makes the True-man kill'd, and saves the Theefe :
     Nay, sometime hangs both Theefe, and True-man : what
     Can it not do, and undoo ?

2   I will make
     One of her women Lawyer to me, for
     I yet not understand the case my selfe .

3   By your leave .

• . . . although it does seem that he occasionally tries to rein himself in, as when trying to work out just how to get to Imogen

> "I know her women are about her : what/If I do line one of their hands,"

one of his very few unembellished moments in the play – though it immediately leads to enormous excesses in his cynical assumption 'Gold' will lead to betrayal anywhere (9/4 the last six lines of F #1)

• and it could be that this intellectual spurt in working things out exhausts him, for the final decision to get 'One of her women Lawyer for me' is, for him, remarkably unreleased (1/1, the last three lines of the speech)

The Tragedie of Cymbeline

Cloten

I am neere to'th'place where they should meet,
4.1.1 - 25

Background: under duress and believing Imogen to be long gone as planned, Pisanio has told Cloten where he had left her: unfortunately, Cloten has journeyed to Wales with nothing but vengeance on his mind - ('unfortunately', for in a moment Cloten is extremely rude to, and challenges, Guiderius/Polidore to a duel, which he loses, and is beheaded as a result)

Style: solo

Where: near the cave of Belarius

To Whom: direct audience address

# of Lines: 24

Probable Timing: 1.15 minutes

Take Note: Cloten's envy/jealousy of Imogen's husband Posthumus is highly emotional, for the three (emotional) semicolons

   " ; I meane,/the Lines of my body are as well drawne as his ; "

   " ; yet this imperseverant/Thing loves him in my despight . "

underscore his murderous intentions.

Cloten

1   I am near to th'place where they should meet,
     if Pisanio have mapp'd it truly .

2   How fit his garments
     serve me !

3   Why should his mistress, who was made by him
     that made the tailor, not be fit too ? the rather (saving
     reverence of the word) for 'tis said a woman's fitness
     comes by fits .

4   Therein I must play the workman .

5   I dare
     speak it to myself, for it is not vainglory for a man,
     and his glass to confer in his own chamber - I mean,
     the lines of my body are as well drawn as his ; no less
     young, more strong, not beneath him in fortunes, be-
     yond him in the advantage of the time, above him in
     birth, alike conversant in general services, and more re-
     markable in single oppositions ; yet this imperseverant
     thing loves him in my despite .

6   What mortality is !

7   Posthumus, thy head, which now is growing upon thy
     shoulders, shall within this hour be off, thy mistress en-
     forced, thy garments cut to pieces before [her] face : and
     all this done, spurn her home to her father, who may
     (happily) be a little angry for my so rough usage ; but my
     Mother, having power of his testiness, shall turn all in-
     to my commendations .

8   My horse is tied up safe, out,
     sword, and to a sore purpose !

9   Fortune put them in to my
     hand !

10   This is the very description of their meeting place,
     and the fellow dares not deceive me .

Cloten

1 I am neere to'th'place where they should meet,
    if Pisanio have mapp'd it truely .

2   How fit his Garments
    serve me ?

3   Why should his Mistris who was made by him
    that made the Taylor, not be fit too ?

4   The rather (saving
    reverence of the Word) for 'tis saide a Womans fitnesse
    comes by fits : therein I must play the Workman, I dare
    speake it to my selfe, for it is not Vainglorie for a man,
    and his Glasse, to confer in his owne Chamber ; I meane,
    the Lines of my body are as well drawne as his ; no lesse
    young, more strong, not beneath him in Fortunes, be-
    yond him in the advantage of the time, above him in
    Birth, alike conversant in generall services, and more re-
    markeable in single oppositions ; yet this imperseverant
    Thing loves him in my despight .

5   What Mortalitie is !

6 Posthumus, thy head (which now is growing uppon thy
    shoulders) shall within this houre be off, thy Mistris in-
    forced, thy Garments cut to peeces before [thy]face : and
    all this done, spurne her home to her Father, who may
    (happily) be a little angry for my so rough usage : but my
    Mother having power of his testinesse, shall turne all in-
    to my commendations .

7   My Horse is tyde up safe, out
    Sword, and to a sore purpose : Fortune put them in to my
    hand : This is the very description of their meeting place
    and the Fellow dares not deceive me .

- though he thinks he is close to achieving both Posthumus' death and the ravishing of Imogen, at the opening of the speech he seems somewhat in control (4/2, F #1-3), though the shortness of the sentences suggest control is somewhat of a struggle for him

- F #4's opening lack of grammar (according to most modern texts) emphasises the crudity of his sexual joke, and the onrush that ensues as he focuses on Posthumus, Cloten becomes much more passionate (13/14 – F #4 through to the first three lines of F #6)

- though the (despairing? bemused?) short-spelled short sentence F #5 summary

  " . What Mortalitie is ! "

  is momentarily intellectual (1/0)

- which immediately dissipates, for the final imagining of his triumph over Imogen is passionate (2/3, the end of F #6)

- yet danger lies in the fact that in checking everything is ready he becomes intellectual once more (5/1, F #7), the move to action enhanced by the fervent surround phrase wish

  " : Fortune put them in to my hand : "

BIBLIOGRAPHY

AND

APPENDICES

The most easily accessible general information is to be found under the citations of *Campbell,* and of *Halliday.* The finest summation of matters academic is to be found within the all-encompassing *A Textual Companion,* listed below in the first part of the bibliography under *Wells, Stanley and Taylor, Gary* (eds.)

Individual modern editions consulted are listed below under the separate headings 'The Complete Works in Compendium Format' and 'The Complete Works in Separate Individual Volumes,' from which the modern text audition speeches have been collated and compiled.

All modern act, scene, and/or line numbers refer the reader to *The Riverside Shakespeare,* in my opinion still the best of the complete works, despite the excellent compendiums that have been published since.

The F/Q material is taken from a variety of already published sources, including not only all the texts listed in the 'Photostatted Reproductions in Compendium Format' below, but also earlier individually printed volumes, such as the twentieth century editions published under the collective title *The Facsimiles of Plays from The First Folio of Shakespeare* by Faber & Gwyer, and the nineteenth century editions published on behalf of The New Shakespere Society.

The heading 'Single Volumes of Special Interest' is offered to newcomers to Shakespeare in the hope that the books may add useful knowledge about the background and craft of this most fascinating of theatrical figures.

PHOTOSTATTED REPRODUCTIONS OF THE ORIGINAL TEXTS IN COMPENDIUM FORMAT

Allen, M.J.B. and K. Muir, (eds.). *Shakespeare's Plays in Quarto.* Berkeley: University of California Press, 1981.

Blaney, Peter (ed.). *The Norton Facsimile (The First Folio of Shakespeare).* New York: W.W.Norton & Co., Inc., 1996 (see also Hinman, below).

Brewer D.S. (ed.). *Mr. William Shakespeare's Comedies, Histories & Tragedies, The Second/Third/Fourth Folio Reproduced in Facsimile.* (3 vols.), 1983.

Hinman, Charlton (ed.). *The Norton Facsimile (The First Folio of Shakespeare)*. New York: W.W.Norton & Company, Inc., 1968.

Kokeritz, Helge (ed.). *Mr. William Shakespeare 's Comedies, Histories & Tragedies*. New Haven: Yale University Press, 1954.

Moston, Doug (ed.). *Mr. William Shakespeare's Comedies, Histories, and Tragedies*. New York: Routledge, 1998.

MODERN TYPE VERSION OF THE FIRST FOLIO IN COMPENDIUM FORMAT

Freeman, Neil. (ed.). *The Applause First Folio of Shakespeare in Modern Type*. New York & London: Applause Books, 2001.

MODERN TEXT VERSIONS OF THE COMPLETE WORKS IN COMPENDIUM FORMAT

Craig, H. and D. Bevington (eds.). *The Complete Works of Shakespeare*. Glenview: Scott, Foresman and Company, 1973.

Evans, G.B. (ed.). *The Riverside Shakespeare*. Boston: Houghton Mifflin Company, 1974.

Wells, Stanley and Gary Taylor (eds.). *The Oxford Shakespeare, William Shakespeare , the Complete Works, Original Spelling Edition,* Oxford: The Clarendon Press, 1986.

Wells, Stanley and Gary Taylor (eds.). *The Oxford Shakespeare, William Shakespeare, The Complete Works, Modern Spelling Edition*. Oxford: The Clarendon Press, 1986.

MODERN TEXT VERSIONS OF THE COMPLETE WORKS IN SEPARATE INDIVIDUAL VOLUMES

The Arden Shakespeare. London: Methuen & Co. Ltd., Various dates, editions, and editors .

Folio Texts. Freeman, Neil H. M. (ed.) Applause First Folio Editions, 1997, and following.

The New Cambridge Shakespeare. Cambridge: Cambridge University Press. Various dates, editions, and editors.

New Variorum Editions of Shakespeare. Furness, Horace Howard (original editor.). New York: 1880, Various reprints. All these volumes have been in a state of re-editing and reprinting since they first appeared in 1880. Various dates, editions, and editors.

The Oxford Shakespeare. Wells, Stanley (general editor). Oxford: Oxford University Press, Various dates and editors.

The New Penguin Shakespeare . Harmondsworth, Middlesex: Penguin Books, Various dates and editors.

The Shakespeare Globe Acting Edition. Tucker, Patrick and Holden, Michael. (eds.). London: M.H.Publications, Various dates.

SINGLE VOLUMES OF SPECIAL INTEREST

Baldwin, T.W. *William Shakespeare's Petty School.* 1943.

Baldwin, T.W. *William Shakespeare's Small wtin and Lesse Greeke.* (2 vols.) 1944.

Barton, John. *Playing Shakespeare.* 1984.

Beckerman, Bernard. *Shakespeare at the Globe, I 599-1609.* 1962. Berryman, John. *Berryman 's Shakespeare.* 1999.

Bloom, Harold. *Shakespeare: The Invention of the Human.* 1998. Booth, Stephen (ed.). *Shakespeare's Sonnets.* 1977.

Briggs, Katharine. *An Encyclopedia of Fairies.* 1976.

Campbell, Oscar James, and Edward G. Quinn (eds.). *The Reader's Encyclopedia of Shakespeare.* 1966.

Crystal, David, and Ben Crystal. *Shakespeare's Words: A Glossary & Language Companion.* 2002.

Flatter, Richard. *Shakespeare's Producing Hand.* 1948 (reprint).

Ford, Boris. (ed.). *The Age of Shakespeare.* 1955.

Freeman, Neil H.M. *Shakespeare's First Texts.* 1994.

Greg, W.W. *The Editorial Problem in Shakespeare: A Survey of the Foundations of the Text.* 1954 (3rd. edition).

Gurr, Andrew . *Playgoing in Shakespeare's London.* 1987. Gurr, Andrew. *The Shakespearean Stage, 1574-1642.* 1987. Halliday, F.E. *A Shakespeare Companion.* 1952.

Harbage, Alfred. *Shakespeare's Audience.* 1941.

Harrison, G.B. (ed.). *The Elizabethan Journals.* 1965 (revised, 2 vols.).

Harrison, G.B. (ed.). *A Jacobean Journal.* 1941.

Harrison, G.B. (ed.). *A Second Jacobean Journal.* 1958.

Hinman, Charlton. *The Printing and Proof Reading of the First Folio of Shakespeare.* 1963 (2 vols.).

Joseph, Bertram. *Acting Shakespeare.* 1960.

Joseph, Miriam (Sister). *Shakespeare's Use of The Arts of wnguage.* 1947.

King, T.J. *Casting Shakespeare's Plays.* 1992.

Lee, Sidney and C.T. Onions. *Shakespeare's England : An Account Of The Life And Manners Of His Age.* (2 vols.) 1916.

Linklater, Kristin. *Freeing Shakespeare's Voice.* 1992.

Mahood, **M .M.** *Shakespeare's Wordplay.* 1957.

O'Connor, Gary. *William Shakespeare: A Popular Life.* 2000.

Ordish, T.F. *Early London Theatres.* 1894. (1971 reprint).

Rodenberg, Patsy. *Speaking Shakespeare.* 2002.

Schoenbaum. S. *William Shakespeare: A Documentary Life.* 1975.

Shapiro, Michael. *Children of the Revels.* 1977.

Simpson, Percy. *Shakespeare's Punctuation.* 1969 (reprint).

Smith, Irwin. *Shakespeare's Blackfriars Playhouse.* 1964.

Southern, Richard. *The Staging of Plays Before Shakespeare.* 1973.

Spevack, M. *A Complete and Systematic Concordance to the Works Of Shakespeare.* 1968-1980 (9vols.).

Tillyard, E.M.W. *The Elizabethan World Picture.* 1942.

Trevelyan, G.M. (ed.). *Illustrated English Social History.* 1942.

Vendler, Helen. *The Art of Shakespeare's Sonnets.* 1999.

Walker, Alice F. *Textual Problems of the First Folio.* 1953.

Walton, J.K. *The Quarto Copy of the First Folio.* 1971.

Warren, Michael. *William Shakespeare, The Parallel King Lear 1608-1623.*

Wells, Stanley and Taylor, Gary (eds.). *Modernising Shakespeare's Spelling, with Three Studies in The Text of Henry V.* 1975.

Wells, Stanley. *Re-Editing Shakespeare for the Modern Reader.* 1984.

Wells, Stanley and Gary Taylor (eds.). *William Shakespeare: A Textual Companion.* 1987.

Wright, George T. *Shakespeare's Metrical Art.* 1988.

HISTORICAL DOCUMENTS

Daniel, Samuel. *The Fowre Bookes of the Civile Warres Between The Howses Of Lancaster and Yorke.* 1595.

Holinshed, Raphael. *Chronicles of England, Scotland and Ireland.* 1587 (2nd. edition).

Halle, Edward. *The Union of the Two Noble and Illustre Famelies of Lancastre And Yorke.* 1548 (2nd. edition).

Henslowe, Philip: Foakes, R.A. and Rickert (eds.). *Henslowe's Diary.* 1961.

Plutarch: North, Sir Thomas (translation of a work in French prepared by Jacques Amyots). *The Lives of The Noble Grecians and Romanes.* 1579.

APPENDIX 1:
GUIDE TO THE EARLY TEXTS

A QUARTO (Q)

A single text, so called because of the book size resulting from a particular method of printing. Eighteen of Shakespeare's plays were published in this format by different publishers at various dates between 1594-1622, prior to the appearance of the 1623 Folio.

THE FIRST FOLIO (F1)'

Thirty-six of Shakespeare's plays (excluding *Pericles* and *Two Noble Kinsmen,* in which he had a hand) appeared in one volume, published in 1623. All books of this size were termed Folios, again because of the sheet size and printing method, hence this volume is referred to as the First Folio. For publishing details see Bibliography, 'Photostated Reproductions of the Original Texts.'

THE SECOND FOLIO (F2)

Scholars suggest that the Second Folio, dated 1632 but perhaps not published until 1640, has little authority, especially since it created hundreds of new problematic readings of its own. Nevertheless more than 800 modern text readings can be attributed to it. The **Third Folio** (1664) and the **Fourth Folio** (1685) have even less authority, and are rarely consulted except in cases of extreme difficulty.

APPENDIX 2:
WORD, WORDS, WORDS

PART ONE: VERBAL CONVENTIONS (AND HOW THEY WILL BE SET IN THE FOLIO TEXT)

"THEN" AND "THAN"

These two words, though their neutral vowels sound different to modern ears, were almost identical to Elizabethan speakers and readers, despite their different meanings. F and Q make little distinction between them, setting them interchangeably . The original setting will be used, and the modern reader should soon get used to substituting one for the other as necessary.

"I," "AY," AND "AYE"

F/Q often print the personal pronoun "I" and the word of agreement "aye" simply as "I." Again, the modern reader should quickly get used to this and make the substitution when necess ary. The reader should also be aware that very occasionally either word could be used and the phrase make perfect sense, even though different meanings would be implied.

"MY SELFE/HIM SELFE/HER SELFE" VERSUS "MYSELF/HIMSELF/HER-SELF"

Generally F/Q separate the two parts of the word, "my selfe" while most modern texts set the single word "myself." The difference is vital, based on Elizabethan philosophy. Elizabethans regarded themselves as composed of two parts, the corporeal "I," and the more spiritual part, the "self." Thus, when an Elizabethan character refers to "my selfe," he or she is often referring to what is to all intents and purposes a separate being, even if that being is a particular part of him- or herself. Thus soliloquies can be thought of as a debate between the "I" and "my selfe," and, in such speeches, even though there may be only one character on-stage, it's as if there were two distinct entities present.

UNUSUAL SPELLING OF REAL NAMES, BOTH OF PEOPLE AND PLACES

Real names, both of people and places, and foreign languages are often reworked for modern understanding. For example, the French town often set in Fl as "Callice" is usually reset as "Calais." F will be set as is.

NON-GRAMMATICAL USES OF VERBS IN BOTH TENSE AND APPLICATION

Modern texts 'correct' the occasional Elizabethan practice of setting a singular noun with plural verb (and vice versa), as well as the infrequent use of the past tense of a verb to describe a current situation. The F reading will be set as is, without annotation.

ALTERNATIVE SETTINGS OF A WORD WHERE DIFFERENT SPELLINGS MAINTAIN THE SAME MEANING

F/Q occasionally set what appears to modern eyes as an archaic spelling of a word for which there is a more common modern alternative, for example "murther" for murder , "burthen" for burden, "moe" for more, "vilde" for vile. Though some modern texts set the Fl (or alternative Q) setting, others modernise. Fl will be set as is with no annotation.

ALTERNATIVE SETTINGS OF A WORD WHERE DIFFERENT SPELLINGS SUGGEST DIFFERENT MEANINGS

Far more complicated is the situation where, while an Elizabethan could substitute one word formation for another and still imply the same thing, to modern eyes the substituted word has an entirely different meaning to the one it has replaced. The following is by no means an exclusive list of the more common dual-spelling, dual-meaning words

anticke-antique	mad-made	sprite-spirit
born-borne	metal-mettle	sun-sonne
hart-heart	mote-moth	travel-travaill
human-humane	pour-(po wre)-power	through-thorough
lest-least	reverent-reverend	troth-truth
lose-loose	right-rite	whether-whither

Some of these doubles offer a metrical problem too, for example "sprite," a one syllable word, versus "spirit." A potential problem occurs in *A Midsummer Nights Dream,* where the modern text s set Q1's "thorough," and thus the scansion pattern of elegant magic can be established, whereas F1's more plebeian "through" sets up a much more awkward and clumsy moment.

The F reading will be set in the Folio Text, as will the modern texts' substitution of a different word formation in the Modern Text. If the modern text substitution has the potential to alter the meaning (and sometimes scansion) of the line, it will be noted accordingly.

PART TWO: WORD FORMATIONS COUNTED AS EQUIVALENTS FOR THE FOLLOWING SPEECHES

Often the spelling differences between the original and modern texts are quite obvious, as with "she"/"shee". And sometimes Folio text passages are so flooded with longer (and sometimes shorter) spellings that, as described in the General Introduction, it would seem that vocally something unusual is taking place as the character speaks.

However, there are some words where the spelling differences are so marginal that they need not be explored any further. The following is by no mean s an exclusive list of word s that in the main will not be taken into account when discussing emotional moments in the various commentaries accompanying the audition speeches.

(modern text spelling shown first)

and- &	murder - murther	tabor - taber
apparent - apparant	mutinous - mutenous	ta'en - tane
briars - briers	naught - nought	then - than
choice - choise	obey - obay	theater - theatre
defense - defence	o'er - o're	uncurrant - uncurrent
debtor - debter	offense - offence	than - then
enchant - inchant	quaint - queint	venomous - venemous
endurance - indurance	reside - recide	virtue - vertue
ere - e'er	Saint - S.	weight - waight
expense - expence	sense - sence	
has - ha's	sepulchre - sepulcher	
heinous - hainous	show - shew	
I'11 - Ile	solicitor - soliciter	
increase - encrease	sugar - suger	

Appendix 2

APPENDIX 3:
THE PATTERN OF MAGIC, RITUAL &
INCANTATION

THE PATTERNS OF "NORMAL" CONVERSATION

The normal pattern of a regular Shakespearean verse line is akin to five pairs of human heart beats, with ten syllables being arranged in five pairs of beats, each pair alternating a pattern of a weak stress followed by a strong stress. Thus, a normal ten syllable heartbeat line (with the emphasis on the capitalised words) would read as

weak- STRONG, weak - STRONG, weak- STRONG, weak- STRONG, weak- STRONG
(shall   I   com-   PARE   thee   TO   a   SUMM-   ers   DAY)

Breaks would either be in length (under or over ten syllables) or in rhythm (any combinations of stresses other than the five pairs of weak-strong as shown above), or both together.

THE PATTERNS OF MAGIC, RITUAL, AND INCANTATION

Whenever magic is used in the Shakespeare plays the form of the spoken verse changes markedly in two ways. The length is usually reduced from ten to just seven syllables, and the pattern of stresses is completely reversed, as if the heartbeat was being forced either by the circumstances of the scene or by the need of the speaker to completely change direction. Thus in comparison to the normal line shown above, or even the occasional minor break, the more tortured and even dangerous magic or ritual line would read as

STRONG - weak, STRONG- weak, STRONG - weak, STRONG
(WHEN   shall   WE   three   MEET   a   GAINE)

The strain would be even more severely felt in an extended passage, as when the three weyward Sisters begin the potion that will fetch Macbeth to them. Again, the spoken emphasis is on the capitalised words and the effort of, and/or fixed determination in, speaking can clearly be felt.

> THRICE the BRINDed CAT hath MEW"D
> THRICE and ONCE the HEDGE-Pigge WHIN"D
> HARPier CRIES, 'tis TIME, 'tis TIME.

UNUSUAL ASPECTS OF MAGIC

It's not always easy for the characters to maintain it. And the magic doesn't always come when the character expects it. What is even more interesting is that while the pattern is found a lot in the Comedies, it is usually in much gentler situations, often in songs *(Two Gentlemen of Verona, Merry Wives of Windsor, Much Ado About Nothing, Twelfth Night, The Winters Tale)* and/or simplistic poetry *(Loves Labours Lost* and *As You Like It)*, as well as the casket sequence in *The Merchant of Venice*.

It's too easy to dismiss these settings as inferior poetry known as doggerel. But this may be doing the moment and the character a great disservice. The language may be simplistic, but the passion and the magical/ritual intent behind it is wonderfully sincere. It's not just a matter of magic for the sake of magic, as with Pucke and Oberon enchanting mortals and Titania. It's a matter of the human heart's desires too. Orlando, in *As You Like It,* when writing peons of praise to Rosalind suggesting that she is composed of the best parts of the mythical heroines because

> THEREfore HEAVen NATure CHARG"D
> THAT one BODie SHOULD be FILL'D
> WITH all GRACes WIDE enLARG"D

And what could be better than Autolycus *(The Winters Tale)* using magic in his opening song as an extra enticement to trap the unwary into buying all his peddler's goods, ballads, and trinkets.

To help the reader, most magic/ritual lines will be bolded in the Folio text version of the speeches.

ACKNOWLEDGMENTS

Neil dedicated *The Applause First Folio in Modern Type*
"To All Who Have Gone Before"
and there are so many who have gone before in the sharing of Shakespeare through publication. Back to John Heminge and Henry Condell who published *Mr. William Shakespeares Comedies, Histories, & Tragedies* which we now know as The First Folio and so preserved 18 plays of Shakespeare which might otherwise have been lost. As they wrote in their note "To the great Variety of Readers.":

> Reade him, therefore; and againe, and againe : And if then you doe not like him, surely you are in some manifest danger, not to understand him. And so we leave you to other of his Friends, whom if you need, can be your guides: if you neede them not, you can lead yourselves, and others, and such readers we wish him.

I want to thank John Cerullo for believing in these books and helping to spread Neil's vision. I want to thank Rachel Reiss for her invaluable advice and assistance. I want to thank my wife, Maren and my family for giving me support, but above all I want to thank Julie Stockton, Neil's widow, who was able to retrive Neil's files from his old non-internet connected Mac, without which these books would not be possible. Thank you Julie.

Shakespeare for Everyone!

Paul Sugarman, April 2021

AUTHOR BIOS

Neil Freeman (1941-2015) trained as an actor at the Bristol Old Vic Theatre School. In the world of professional Shakespeare he acted in fourteen of the plays, directed twenty-four, and coached them all many times over.

His groundbreaking work in using the first printings of the Shakespeare texts in performance, on the rehearsal floor and in the classroom led to lectures at the Shakespeare Association of America and workshops at both the ATHE and VASTA, and grants/fellowships from the National Endowment for the Arts (USA), The Social Science and Humanities Research Council (Canada), and York University in Toronto. He prepared and annotated the thirty-six individual Applause First Folio editions of Shakespeare's plays and the complete *The Applause First Folio of Shakespeare in Modern Type*. For Applause he also compiled *Once More Unto the Speech, Dear Friends*, three volumes (Comedy, History and Tragedy) of Shakespeare speeches with commentary and insights to inform audition preparation.

He was Professor Emeritus in the Department of Theatre, Film and Creative Writing at the University of British Columbia, and dramaturg with The Savage God project, both in Vancouver, Canada. He also taught regularly at the National Theatre School of Canada, Concordia University, Brigham Young University.. He had a Founder's Ring (and the position of Master Teacher) with Shakespeare & Company in Lenox, Mass: he was associated with the Will Geer Theatre in Los Angeles; Bard on the Beach in Vancouver; Repercussion Theatre in Montreal; and worked with the Stratford Festival, Canada, and Shakespeare Santa Cruz.

Paul Sugarman is an actor, editor, writer, and teacher of Shakespeare. He is founder of the Instant Shakespeare Company, which has presented annual readings of all of Shakespeare's plays in New York City for over twenty years. For Applause Theatre & Cinema Books, he edited John Russell Brown's publication of *Shakescenes: Shakespeare for Two* and The Applause Shakespeare Library, as well as Neil Freeman's Applause First Folio Editions and *The Applause First Folio of Shakespeare in Modern Type*. He has published pocket editions of all of Shakespeare's plays using the original settings of the First Folio in modern type for Puck Press. Sugarman studied with Kristin Linklater and Tina Packer at Shakespeare & Company where he met Neil Freeman.